# Hugh Johnson's
# How to Enjoy Your Wine

# Hugh Johnson's
# How to Enjoy Your Wine

GRAMERCY BOOKS
NEW YORK

Copyright © 1985, 1998 Octopus Publishing Group Ltd

Text copyright © 1985, 1998 Hugh Johnson

Revised 1998

Reprinted 1999, 2001

This 2006 edition is published by Gramercy Books, an imprint of Random House Value Publishing, a division of Random House, Inc., New York, by arrangement with Mitchell Beazley, an imprint of Octopus Publishing Group, Ltd, London.

Gramercy is a registered trademark and the colophon is a trademark of Random House, Inc.

Random House
New York • Toronto • London • Sydney • Auckland
www.randomhouse.com

Executive Art Editor: Fiona Knowles
Editor: Diane Pengelly
Production: Rachel Lynch
Index: Marie Lorimer

Printed and bound in China

A catalog record for this title is available from the Library of Congress.

ISBN 0-517-22747-9

10 9 8 7 6 5 4 3 2 1

# Contents

# The art of enjoyment

D on't look at the label. Ignore (for the moment) even the price. Let yourself be guided by one thing: how much do you like what you have in your glass? This is rule one of enjoying wine, but perhaps more easily stated than applied. 'How do you know how much you like it?' is far from being a dumb question.

The extremes of wine's myriad identities, from most delicate white to most unctuous amber, are as far apart as Alps and desert, sonnet and epic, Chopin and Wagner, crocus and rhododendron. The imagery is far-flown, but that precisely is what makes wine different from anything else we drink. It ranges from lace to leather, from glossy to gritty, from insinuating to explosive, in keys, colours and tones innumerable. So how much do you like it?

A wise man once defined a connoisseur (funny old-fashioned word) as someone who can tell good wine from bad and is able to enjoy the different merits of different wines. Two phases, then: judgement – is it good nor not? And appreciation – seeing the flavour in context, comparing it with similar and dissimilar flavours, speculating about who made it, where and when. And most important just rolling it round your gums, becoming aware of fruit and structure, light and shade, depth, texture and astringency; what you see, what you smell, what crosses your palate and finally leaves (or doesn't leave) its imprint, its phantom flavour, after it has gone.

You can be a technical taster. Makers and traders of wine are condemned, poor souls, to put names to every nuance they detect, to worry about latent faults and not-so-latent price rises. But you are much better advised to drink in simple attentive appreciation.

From mere rain percolating through the soil the roots have collected, the vine transported, the leaves ripened and the grapes matured this magic juice. The yeasts on their bloomy skins have seized on it for food, converting its sugar into alcohol, starting a process of infinite complexity which will end only when the wine is drunk.

I have every sympathy with drivers who don't know what goes on under the bonnet of their car. Much less with drinkers who never pause to taste what they are drinking. Good wine is as close as we can come to imbibing the very nature of a specific spot on the earth's surface. Do you need to be a mystic to find the prospect at least intriguing? When you learn, as you soon do, that the taste, and hence the pleasure, can change within a stone's throw, the mystery begins to seep into you. Don't fight it. There are too few direct links between nature and art.

# Opening the bottle

*A preliminary briefing on corks, capsules and
containers, together with a description of the weapons
used in getting at the wine and the emergency measures
that must sometimes be resorted to.*

I t has taken centuries – over 60 of them – to develop the
perfect container for wine. Now we have it, the greatest
invention of the 17th century: the bottle and cork.

A wine bottle is not just a container. It is a sealed vessel
in which the wine, protected from the air, holds its complex
potencies in readiness for the day when it is drunk. Once the
bottle is opened the wine is exposed to the destructive
effects of oxygen. There is no going back.

Pulling a cork therefore always has a touch of drama
about it; sometimes more than a touch when the cork is
unwilling to yield to muscle and corkscrew.

To take an extreme case first, here is what you do if the
cork proves totally immovable. Take the heaviest kitchen
knife you can find. Hold the bottle in one hand, with the neck
pointing away from you, and the knife in the other, with the
blunt edge toward the bottle. Now run the blade up the neck
as hard has you can, hitting the 'collar' of the bottle with a
terrific whack, and the neck should break off cleanly.
Ridiculous? Strange to say it is almost routine in some of the
more swagger Champagne houses, where they use a sabre.
(A hussar uniform helps, too.) But practise first. Your dinner
guests will never forget it.

*Above: A scene intimately connected with almost every bottle of wine you have ever drunk: the unique cork oaks of Iberia. Cork-making is a laborious business* which many argue has no realistic bearing on most everyday wines. Expect to see more and more alternatives, from plastic to screw-caps.

## Corks: the first hurdle

Why are all fine wines plugged with what amounts to a lump of wood – or at least tree bark? It sounds unnecessarily primitive. The fact is that there is nothing to touch cork for the qualities that make it an ideal wine plug. It is light, clean and almost impermeable. It is smooth, yet stays firmly in position in the neck of the bottle. It does not expand or contract with changes in temperature, it rarely rots and does not burn easily. Above all it is highly elastic. Squeeze it into the neck of a bottle using a corking machine and it will immediately expand to make an airtight and watertight fit.

What is this material that has proved such a boon to the wine
trade – and can be such a strain on the muscles? Briefly, cork
is the outer bark of the cork oak, *Quercus suber*, which
grows most abundantly in Spain and Portugal. Before its bark
is harvested, a cork tree must grow for 20 years; then the
bark can be stripped about once in every decade. The sheets
of bark are subjected to a long process of drying, treating
with fungicide and storing before they are ready to be cut
into those familiar plugs. A normal-sized cork is 24mm ($^{15}/_{16}$in)
in diameter and will be squeezed into an 18mm ($^{23}/_{32}$in) neck.
Champagne corks (31mm/1¼in for a 17.5mm $^{11}/_{16}$in neck) are
made from three layers of cork glued together, and a third of
the cork bulges out over the top of the neck like the head of
a mushroom. Cheaper corks are made from an agglomeration
of dust and scraps.

Corks also vary in length. Basically, the longer a wine
needs to be stored, the longer the cork. Many corks have
information about the wine stamped on them – sometimes just
the name of the region where the wine was made, sometimes
almost as much detail as on the label.

Once in position, a good cork will last at least 25 years and
sometimes as long as 50, although the best cellars will recork
their old vintages at 25-year intervals. Only slowly will the
cork become brittle and crumbly. It is essential, however, that
the cork be kept wet by constant contact with the wine in the
bottle. This is why wine bottles are always kept lying down.

Occasionally a small amount of fungus escapes the
sterilization process and remains in the cork. When the
infected part is in contact with the contents of the bottle the
wine picks up the smell – a simple whiff of mould. Such a

wine is said to be 'corky' or 'corked'. A rare problem, but when it happens there is no alternative but to jettison the bottle and open another one.

Any bottle of wine you buy will have the cork covered by a so-called capsule – partly for neatness or ornament, partly to

**Above:** *The original functions of the capsule were to protect the rim of the bottle and to keep the cork clean. This array of vintage bottles displays a variety of the materials used: sheet lead (the old standard), modern aluminium alloy, sealing wax, a screw cap, thin metal foil and a tear-off cap (for truly ordinary wine). Some old Spanish bottles even have gold mesh to enhance the sense that the content is precious. In future we are likely to see even more variations as corks are superseded for all but fine wines.*

protect the rim from being chipped and the cork from getting dirty (or even eaten by mice). The best-quality capsules were formerly made of thin sheet lead, painted and usually embossed. Modern thinking is that lead is a pollutant; even a poison. Hence the aluminium alloy of today's capsules – which in turn produces another danger: beware of cutting your finger. Some people like to take just the top of the capsule off, leaving the rest to decorate the bottle. I usually do this with the tall flasks that hold German or German-style wines – and often with any wine that I am going to put on the table in its own bottle. If I am going to decant, on the other hand, I always cut the capsule right off so that I can really see what I am doing.

Originally capsules were made by dipping the business end of the bottle in sealing wax. That's why some old corkscrews had a hammer-handle for chipping off the wax and a brush for getting rid of the messy debris. If you find yourself dealing with an old wax seal, take my advice and remove it over the kitchen sink or outside the back door – some place where chips of old wax won't matter.

The most attractive capsules of all are made by dipping the corked neck in beeswax; still the custom with the finest Hungarian Tokays.

Cheap wines today occasionally have plastic capsules. I hate them, not only for being plastic but also for being the devil to cut off. Some have perforated strips and tags, but these usually break off, so that you are left having to gouge off the plastic with a knife. Aluminium foil is another cheap capsule material used for bargain-basement wines. At least it has the advantage of being easy to remove.

Then of course there is the screw-cap. Traditionalists may shudder and swear that a cork is the only stopper for a fine wine, but the modern screw-cap is a perfect hygienic and airtight closure – and it has the tremendous advantage that you can easily put it back on again. For standard brands there is a lot to be said for screw-caps. Whether they will ever be used for fine wines is a topical debate. Logic says yes; sentiment no. Most wine-drinkers are deeply attached to corks and corkscrews as part of the ritual that distinguishes wine from other drinks.

The supply of good cork is finite, though. We are going to see more and more artificial corks of various kinds. Already there is one on the market that needs no corkscrew: it has a sort of plunger built in. Expect to see plastic imitation corks on many, if not most, lower-price wines in the fairly near future.

No harm will come to any wine (except maybe very old wine) if you recork it and keep it in the refrigerator for a while. Most wines, red or white but especially white, have a much longer refrigerator-life than most people realize. One or two days carry very little risk, and I have come back to a bottle after a week to find it has lost nothing. The trick is to cut the top (the thinner end) off the original cork to get a clean end, and then drive it back in upside down with your fist.

To keep the fizz in Champagne there are many ingenious expanding bungs. Alternatively, there is a simple piece of jiggery-pokery you can do by inserting the handle of a small silver teaspoon into the bottle – why this keeps the bubbles in is something I have never fathomed.

**Above:** *Ingenuity in engineering has been stretched to the limit applying pull to corks. The story starts (centre row, far right) with the back-breaking straight pull. Next to it is the 'Ah-so', or Butler's Friend, which removes the cork slyly, without piercing it, so no-one would know. All the others apply some sort of counter-pressure to the bottle, from the zigzag (top left) to the ever-popular Waiter's Friend (bottom, second from left) whose 'claw' grips the lip of the bottle, the 'hypodermic' which blows out the cork, and (bottom right) the last word – so far – the Screwpull in one of its several guises.*

# Corkscrews: choosing and using

The essentially simple act of opening a wine bottle can be
turned into an elaborate performance. Some waiters, for
example, make a fetish out of holding the bottle in a
gleaming white napkin – a wise precaution in the days when
bottles sometimes broke during opening, but hardly
necessary today. A sommelier trying to make an impression
can spend five minutes on the simple act of getting a cork
out. You and I, though, have better things to do.

First remove the capsule, or cut it clear of the lip. Then if
necessary give the lip and the top of the cork a quick wipe to
remove any dirt or mould – here's where a cloth comes in
handy. Insert the corkscrew, not driving it right through so
that it pushes bits of cork into the wine (not that they do any
harm; they are simply not pretty). Now draw the cork with a
slow steady pull. A well-designed corkscrew works on the
lever principle, using the bottle-lip as the fulcrum. Models
such as the Screwpull, the Waiter's Friend or the Butterfly
Lever remove most of the effort from the operation. Keep the
cork if you are planning to drink only part of the bottle and
store the rest in the refrigerator. Finally, you may want to use
your cloth again to give a last wipe around the inside of the
rim. That's it – you're ready to pour the first glass.

## Corks that break or won't budge

Occasionally corks are too tight and break up (especially if
the corkscrew is badly designed). Or they may have grown
crumbly with age and need kid-glove treatment. Then again,
they may be too loose and get pushed in, at which point you
are rewarded with a wine fountain and a sticky arm.

What if a cork comes to pieces? One technique worth trying, to remove a fragment out of reach in the neck, is to put the screw in again at the most oblique angle you have room for, then push toward the side of the neck at the same time as pulling upwards. You squeeze the cork against the glass and hold it in one piece while gently pulling it out.

If that fails, and you are left with a cork in pieces in the neck and fragments floating in the wine, you might as well push the rest in. There is a fairly effective device made of three pieces of wire which will retrieve the bigger bits of cork easily enough from bottles with sloping shoulders. If it's a Bordeaux-type bottle with more pronounced shoulders, simply pour past them. You will get cork in your wine – at least in the first glass – but never mind; it won't affect the taste.

## Opening vintage port with fire and feather

Vintage port is in a category of its own. The bottles are designed to be stored for many years to allow time for the raw grape juice and brandy to 'marry' and mellow. There is still a convention (more honoured in the breach than the observance) of laying down a case of port when a son is born, to be drunk when he grows up.

The neck of a vintage port bottle is tall and slightly bulging, and is fitted with a very long cork. If the bottle is stored for longer than about 25 years the cork can become soft and crumbly, tending to break up when you pull on it with the corkscrew. In this condition it is virtually impossible to extract in the normal way. Sometimes the technique of inserting the corkscrew at an angle will work; usually it just makes a mess. More extreme measures are required.

**Above:** *Would anyone really use red-hot tongs to open a bottle of wine? They sound a desperate measure. In fact they are a well-tried way when the long cork in an ancient bottle of vintage port has become too crumbly for a corkscrew. First the tongs are heated in an open fire or in a gas flame.*

**Above:** *When the orange glow confirms that the tongs are hot enough, they are clamped firmly around the neck of the waiting bottle. They should be positioned just above the bottom of the cork – clear of the wine – and held tight shut for at least half a minute to heat a ring of glass.*

**Above:** *Remove the tongs and lay them aside as swiftly as possible. Then stroke the bottle neck just where the tongs encircled it with a feather that has been dipped in cold water (a damp cloth will do). The sudden change of temperature causes the neck to crack right through in a clean ring.*

**Above:** *Finally you take a firm grip of the top of the neck and lift the whole thing neatly off, as easily as a stopper. The cork, still intact and just protruding from the bottle top, will have prevented any glass from falling into the wine – but usually the glass has split so cleanly that there are no chips.*

You can, of course, take a cutlass to it. But a less violent and more elegant way is to use a pair of 'port tongs' (of the kind shown on page 17). You heat them in an open fire or gas flame until they are red hot, clamp them around the neck of the bottle and leave them there for half a minute. Then wipe the same spot with a damp cloth or – for a touch of style – a feather dipped in water. A faint snapping sound will be heard, and you will know that the neck has split in a neat circle. Then you just lift off the top like a stopper, bringing, unless you are unlucky, the whole cork with it. An impressive trick – but the main thing is that it works.

# Storing the wine

*All you ever really needed to know about keeping a
wine cellar – even in a wardrobe. Why, when and
for how long to store wine. An unfamiliar use for a
can of hairspray. And how to remember where
you have put which bottle.*

D o you mean I can't open it now? That depends. Any wine
that's worth a premium is worth storing, at least for a
few months, and maybe for years. In simplest terms, the
better the wine the more there is to gain from patience.

The thing to remember is that wine is alive – if you ever
meet a dead wine you will know it without being told. Being
alive, it reacts to certain physical stimuli (such as violent
movements and extreme heat and cold). It also passes at a

*Above: Few discussions in wine are
more difficult than when to open the last
relic bottle of a great vintage. At the
Bordeaux First Growth Château Margaux*
*there are remnants of vintages 150
years old. Perfectly stored and never
moved, the wine will probably be at least
sound, however faded.*

faster or slower rate through the process of ageing. The mark of the best wine is that it has the longest life span – given that it is kept in suitable conditions.

Everyday wine, the bulk stuff, is blended to be at the best age for drinking (usually very young) when it is bottled. Good examples of everyday wine are robust enough to live on happily for, say, six months to a year. In fact, really well-chosen everyday wines can show a distinct touch of class if they are given a chance by being carefully stored for a year or so.

Don't assume, though, that old jug is better than new jug. The opposite is more likely to be true. But if a jug red strikes you as being unusually tasty for the category where most reds are fairly thin, give a few bottles a chance to prove themselves. Instead of opening them in quick succession drink them at intervals of say, a month or six weeks. You will soon be aware whether you are watching improvement or decline – and drink the rest or keep it accordingly.

I would hesitate to keep low-price whites on the same principle. Freshness (if they have it) is often their main virtue, so don't miss it. Buy them only as you drink them.

At the premium level things are, or should be, different. Whenever you pay more for a distinct style, whether it is an *Appellation Contrôlée* or something from a highly regarded winery, you are paying for extra flavour, extra strength and vitality, extra nuance.

In living wine these qualities are rarely predictable. For several months after bottling, fine wines are often in a sort of state of dumb shock. They seem to sulk. Open them then and you will be disappointed by the lack of fragrance and flavour. It is worth, therefore, keeping all newly made and bottled fine wines for at least two or three months before even sampling them. As living creatures they can suffer. Shipping them a distance to your home can give them the sulks almost as much as the original bottling can. Mature wines don't need such a long recovery period as new ones, but try to give them a few weeks' rest at least.

Beaujolais Nouveau is generally held to be the great exception: at its best for breakfast the day after bottling (and in the heady days of the Beaujolais race, a helicopter ride into the bargain). Don't believe the myth. There is no doubt that good Beaujolais Nouveau – which almost by definition means Beaujolais-Villages Nouveau – improves steadily through Christmas and the whole of its first winter. Just see how silky it is at Easter and you will realise what you would have missed by drinking it all in the autumn.

The rewards for storing the grander grades of wine increase in direct proportion to their initial quality. First Growths are traded, as well as drunk, because they are known to have the potential to live, gradually improving, developing and finally (when rarity adds to their value) declining over a period that can last anything between ten and 100 years.

## Keeping a cellar

Though nothing can quite equal either the atmosphere or the efficacy of an ancient underground cellar, cool, dark and tranquil, all beams and cobwebs, the word and the fact today are usually interpreted in terms of some cramped, often pretty makeshift, space above ground. What is important, and what still makes a hole in the ground the best of all places to store wine, is the unchanging conditions in a cellar: a cool, even temperature, dark, calm and a certain degree of humidity. With ingenuity these conditions can be achieved in a cupboard under the stairs, in the back of a garage ... anywhere in fact that can be insulated. Most modern wine cellars are contrived in less-than-ideal conditions. But don't be put off. Given reasonable consideration most wines survive.

The first requirement is that the wines be kept at a reasonably even temperature, neither too warm nor too cold, but somewhat below normal room temperature. This means anything between 7–18°C (45–64°F). The ideal is about 10°C (50°F). At 10°C your white wines will be kept constantly at the right temperature for serving, and the red ones will mature slowly but steadily.

*Above: Cellar mould is a specific fungus,* Cladosporium cellarii, *which flourishes in certain damp cellar conditions, apparently nourished by the trace of* alcohol in the atmosphere. It is at its most dramatic in the tufa tunnels where Tokay is matured, sometimes engulfing old bottles completely.

Slow and moderate fluctuations in temperature will not harm the wines, but sudden and violent changes will age them prematurely.

Darkness is important because light will age a wine before its time, especially if it is in a clear glass bottle – and ultraviolet rays will penetrate even a dark-tinted bottle. This is why, incidentally, you should never buy a fine wine off a brightly lit shelf in a store.

Moderate humidity keeps a cork in a good, pliable, resilient condition and stops it from shrinking. If your storage room is unduly dry you can install a humidifier or improvise one in the form of a bowl of moist sand.

Too much humidity will not damage the wine, but it soon rots cardboard boxes and encourages mould on labels. The label is the gauge of the value of a bottle; you can't afford to let it moulder. If this may be a problem there is a simple solution: before you store a bottle give the label a squirt with some scentless hair lacquer or artist's fixative. Either makes a reasonably permanent seal against damp.

The cellar should not suffer from the shakes. Calm repose without vibration is ideal for wine. In practice this is unlikely to be a problem in most homes. The small vibrations encountered in an average house do no harm.

Let us suppose that your dwelling, like most people's, is cellar-less (in the traditional sense). How do you set about creating the best storage conditions for your wine? Your first problem is likely to be space. If you live in your own house it is sometimes possible to have a small cellar dug out – say under the floor of your garage. A pre-cast concrete spiral cellar, ready to be sunk like a well under the floor, is an

***Above:*** *A spiral cellar built of precast concrete modules is an imaginative and highly practical answer for houses with no good wine storage space. It can be installed relatively simply (this one was accommodated by excavating beneath the garage floor) and provide true cellar conditions.*

ingenious and excellent solution – if not a cheap one. Failing some such investment, you will have to make do with any available space where conditions are approximately right. Ideally you should find a small room or cupboard without an outside wall and insulate it generously. A fireplace with a blocked-up chimney is a possible solution. Limited in space, though. The bottom of a wardrobe might do at a pinch. A much better solution is a temperature-controlled storage unit: a kind of refrigerator about 4°C (39°F) warmer than the normal. EuroCave is a principal maker (the name has largely been adopted as the generic for such appliances). For wine drinkers who have small apartments these are surely the best answer. A traditional wine merchant will usually store (for a small fee) wine you have bought that won't fit into the cabinet, until you have room for it. The step beyond (and may you reach it soon) is an insulated, air-conditioned room.

*Left: The EuroCave is probably the leader among brands of what might be called 'wine fridges'. These are designed to provide long-term storage at thermostatically-controlled temperatures and can include separate sections – for example a 'cold compartment' where Champagne can be kept at the ready.*

## Keeping track of your stock

It's a fair bet that once you have put a bottle away you will forget which slot you put it in. If you are to use your precious storage space with any efficiency at all a bit of book-keeping is essential. It needn't be difficult. Just mark each row and column of your wine rack with a number or letter (say, numbers horizontally, letters vertically). Each aperture will have, as it were, a grid reference consisting of a letter and a number. Whenever you store a bottle simply

**Above:** *This wine rack is arranged on a space-saving grid system marked with the letters A to F vertically, numbers one to 12 horizontally. When a bottle is stored in its pigeonhole its grid-reference is entered in the cellar notebook alongside its name, making it a straightforward matter to find it again.*

write this reference in your notebook (and cross it out when you drink the bottle). With such a system you can even scatter a dozen bottles of one wine all over the cellar, wherever there happens to be a vacant slot, and find them all again easily. Any other method wastes precious space.

*In this rack six dozen bottles are visible, but it is double-depth so can accommodate two bottles end-to-end where necessary, giving it a storage capacity of 144 bottles. It is clear which compartments are full and which have more room: where there is a 'back' bottle, the front one extends slightly further out.*

# How long must I keep it?

Although it is certainly true that far more good wines are drunk too early in their lives than too late, it is a bitter moment when you open a bottle and find it 'over the hill', faded, dried-out or flattened by age. Like missing a plane – except that another won't come along. So how long should you keep it?

There never was, and never will be, a cut-and-dried answer. The better sort of vintage chart tells you, in general terms, when each vintage of each important region is nearing maturity. My *Pocket Wine Book* (in the USA *The Pocket Encyclopedia of Wine*) goes into wine-by-wine detail annually for some 6,000 individual wines. But let us suppose you have had a bottle for three, or five, or ten years and you want to know whether there is any advantage in keeping it longer. Read the charts, read the wine magazines. But also look at the bottle.

Red wines reveal a lot about themselves by their colour, even through the glass of the bottle. Young wines are clearly red or purple, varying in intensity from vintage to vintage, region to region and grape variety to variety.

If a red wine is impenetrably dark when held against a light bulb, the odds are that the flavour will be impenetrably intense, young and (maybe) harsh. Look at a few bottles against the light and you will quickly learn that young Bordeaux, for example, is usually much darker than young burgundy. Look at ten-year-old bottles of both and you will see how both have faded away from purple and toward red-brown. Prime time for good wines is usually when the wine is just moving across the spectrum of red into faint hints of brown or orange.

*Below and below right:* The variations in wine colour are produced by many factors. Grape variety is one: red burgundy and all Pinot Noirs are (or should be) always lighter in tone

than Bordeaux and other wines made from the thicker-skinned Cabernet Sauvignon grape. The difference is plainly visible if you compare a bottle of each held up to a light bulb.

*Below and below right:* While red wine colour steadily fades with age, from purplish through red to orange, the colour of white wines develops in the opposite direction. The glass on the

left below is a young dry wine; that on the right is either a mature dry white or – more probably – a sweet wine tinted toward gold by the action of botrytis on the grape skins.

White wines move the other way – from very pale to straw to gold to amber. Only such noble sweet wines as Sauternes and Tokay should ever be kept beyond the transition from straw to gold – which is easy to see through the (usually clear glass) Sauternes bottle. Respect a fine white wine's pedigree, and give it at least a year, preferably two or three – but then drink it. Only a great white burgundy, a Corton-Charlemagne or a Grand Cru Chablis, or a Spätlese or Auslese from a top German grower, calls for the ten-year treatment. But do believe what you read about the finest wines – red or white. It is a crying shame to drink them while they are still pubescent.

## Stacks and racks

Old-fashioned cellars were designed with so-called 'bins' – simple shelves on which you piled the bottles as many as ten deep, because you bought your wine by the barrel and it was all the same. Even the label is a relatively new invention. A case of port delivered to my cellar back in 1965 had no labels. The shipper was identified only by the embossed end of the capsule. Each bottle just had a white paint mark to show which way up it should be. You can – indeed you should – use a label in the same way: keep the label uppermost and any sediment will be at the bottom when you come to pouring. You will also be able to read it easily.

The trouble with using the bin method today is that we don't buy vast quantities of one wine – indeed, few of us buy vast quantities at all. We may perhaps have only one bottle of a particular wine, and we need to be able to winkle out individual bottles easily. So we need racks.

*Above:* When I constructed this rack in my cellar, intending it to be as versatile as possible, I foolishly made the apertures too small to hold full dozens.

Finding the wine you are looking for can turn into something of a treasure hunt, but the system does have one advantage: it will hold magnums.

A rack is simply a structure with a series of pigeon-holes, each hole capable of holding one or more bottles. Racks with one-bottle apertures are the most useful all-rounders. Another model is deep enough to allow two bottles to be placed end to end in each aperture. You can mislay bottles in the back of these and come across them as a pleasant surprise months (in my case sometimes years) later.

The commonest and best type of manufactured wine rack is made of wooden bars connected by galvanized metal strips in a modular system. There are any number of ways you can make your own bottle rack or improvise one. Short lengths of drainpipe are a practical and easy dodge. Wooden wine-cases are too good to throw away; they can be adapted. Even one of the ordinary cardboard boxes wine arrives in can make quite a serviceable temporary rack, provided of course that the room is dry.

## Space-age cellar

The closest thing to a perfect cellar must be the Aladdin's cave of a celebrated collector of rare wine I am glad to call a friend, in southern California. It is airy, cool, humidity-controlled, immaculately ordered – and huge. There is room for 40,000 bottles of all sizes, including special racks for every size from half-bottles to the largest, Impériales and Nebuchadnezzars. The wines range in age over about 100 years – with few, except perhaps Champagne, intended for immediate drinking. It is a cellar for browsing, daydreaming, gloating if you like: an ideally designed repository for the finest wines, where their qualities are carefully recorded, along with the opinions of all who taste them.

What are we to learn from this extravagant model? First, to plan ahead: to make calculations about what wines we will want (and can afford) to drink in their maturity. Forty thousand bottles is far more than the owner will ever drink. Much of it is therefore an investment for resale when it reaches maturity. Its impeccable provenance will guarantee that it fetches the best price.

The second lesson is one of orderliness and book-keeping. Not to be able to find a wine is bad. Not to be able to remember what it was like after you have tasted it is equally irritating. Cellar records should lead you straight to the bottle you are looking for, and remind you of when you last tasted it, and what you and your friends thought of it. They can also record where you bought it (and why), its price, what food you have eaten with it, what reference books and magazines have said about it, who you have drunk it with, and when you consider it should reach its full maturity or start to decline and need drinking.

*Above: A traditional domestic wine cellar, its 'bins' dating from the 18th century, can come to have a friendly lived-in look, with wooden cases used for* extra storage, bottles standing up ready for consumption, a wicker basket to carry them upstairs and some memorable empties hanging about too.

# Decanting and serving

*The art of decanting (without the cant).*
*Should wine breathe or not breathe? How to use*
*an ice bucket – or a wet newspaper instead.*
*And a word about glasses, good and bad.*

The first English dictionary defined a decanter as "a glass vessel for pouring off a liquid clear from its lees". Wine, in those days, was expected to be a bit murky at the bottom, whether in barrel or bottle. You decanted it into an elegant vessel for the table so your guests could admire its·colour and clarity. Then you hung a label of silver or enamel around its neck to proclaim its contents. It all added up to dressing your wine to look its best at dinner – a procedure made less necessary today by clean-limbed bottles and eloquent paper labels.

*Left and far left: Decanters can be some of the most beautiful of wine artefacts. Both these are modern reproductions of classic shapes from late 18th- and early 19th-century England, the time when decanter design was at its most assured: elegant, simple and practical. Far left is a 'mallet' or 'club' decanter, delicately engraved. Left is a 'three ring decanter' (the rings are for a steady grip) with a 'bull's eye' stopper. This is my favourite model.*

Why, then, do we still decant? More to the point, why is it the
modern custom to decant the best wines; those with the
proudest labels? Mumbo jumbo and a surprising amount of
acrimony surround what seems a very straightforward
operation. It is the quickest way of starting an argument
among wine buffs. Should you or shouldn't you decant
wine X? If so, when?

Dr Johnson's original definition still points the way. If a
bottle of wine has 'lees' or sediment (which nowadays comes
only with age) it needs decanting. If you pour it from the
original bottle, each backward and forward tilt as you go
from glass to glass stirs up the muck and mixes it with the
clear wine. In a bad case, especially with old red burgundy
(burgundy can have very fine lees) as much as half the bottle
will be thick and unpalatable unless you pour it carefully, in
one uninterrupted movement, into a decanter.

The arguments start over what other effects decanting
has on the wine. Pouring it from its bottle into a broader
vessel, where it lies with a wide surface open to the air
(whether or not there is a stopper), radically increases its
access to oxygen. In its own bottle it has been oxygen-
starved. Now suddenly all its components can breathe in all
the oxygen they have been missing. It would be surprising if
there were not a fairly rapid change of scent and flavour.

Yet in most instances there is very little. Some authorities
find themselves unable to tell any difference at all. Others
(and this is the conventional French view) say they notice a
slight decline in the vigour and personality of the wine. If a
Frenchman decants wine at all it is usually just before
drinking it. In a sense, he regards his glass as the decanter.

An equally well-established, specifically British, custom is purposely to expose wine to the air by decanting it several hours before drinking. The effect depends, as you would expect, on the age and quality of the wine. Young reds being drunk before time has had its mellowing effect, still aggressive with tannin and acidity, tend to lose their bite and drink more smoothly. Mature ones give off more fragrance after a while in the decanter than when the bottle was opened. Low-quality wines have little to gain, but you may just get a bit more of whatever they have to offer, for better or worse. High-quality wines tend to develop their 'bouquet' slowly – but then they have much more to lose if they are opened too long before drinking. The key question, with no steady answer, is: at what point does the expensive fragrance, which is intended for your nostrils, begin to dissipate itself upon the ungrateful air?

I am certain (which is not to say that everyone is) that no harm can come to vigorous young wine of good quality (say a five-year-old Bordeaux of a good vintage) by being decanted up to four or five hours before it is to be drunk – which is very convenient when you are making preparations for a dinner party. You can open the wine, taste it, decant it and think about its proper temperature well in advance of guests' arrival. I wouldn't even hesitate to decant such a wine at lunch time and leave it, with the stopper in, until the evening.

Real uncertainty starts with precious relics. It would be a shame to miss any of the perfumes that arise like incense from a classic wine in full maturity. This is the best argument for the French approach. If your friends are as intrigued as you are, you can go on finding different redolences for hours.

If a question-mark continues to hang over the subject it is because even decanting-sceptics admit that the last glass, even of an old wine, is often more thrilling than the first. In a really extreme case a century-old Château Lafite, opened at nine in the evening, seemed a mere relic at dinner. But what little was left in the decanter at breakfast the next morning was a miracle of intricate sweetness. One thing is sure: the argument will continue.

## Getting the temperature right

If there is one single factor that makes or mars your full enjoyment of any wine it is its temperature in your glass. The ideal temperature depends on the weather as well as the wine. In summer all wines taste better a few degrees colder than they do in winter. The one cardinal rule is that any wine should be refreshing.

For most white wines, perfect storage temperature (the chill of a cellar – or indeed a EuroCave) is ideal for drinking too. The kitchen refrigerator at around 7°C (44°F) is a

*Left: Although a silver ice bucket cannot honestly be said to be essential for cool wine it adds an air of go-for-it glamour as nothing else does. Especially when it is an (exceedingly rare) magnum cooler such as the one on the left in the picture. The trick is to fill it with half ice and half cold water. A handful of salt in the ice lowers the temperature further.*

shade too cold for most white wines – except in summer when they will rapidly warm up anyway. In any case a refrigerator is a very inefficient way of chilling, simply because air is a bad conductor of heat.

For the same reason a bucket full of ice on its own is also inefficient. The one really effective way of extracting the calories is total immersion in water and ice together, since water is the perfect conductor. Bear in mind that small ice cubes will melt quickly. The bigger the block of ice you use, the longer it will last. An ice bucket should be deep enough to immerse the whole bottle. If it isn't, put the neck in first, then reverse the bottle after a few minutes. Eight minutes in icy water will cool a bottle from 18 to 13°C (65 to 55°F). In a normal refrigerator those few degrees would take an hour to get rid of.

Once the bottle is cold there are some very pretty containers to keep it cool on the table. I have an Italian earthenware one that works like an old milk cooler. You soak it in water first, and evaporation keeps it cool. There is also a clear plastic insulated model that works on the principle that cold air (off the bottle) lies on the bottom – more pretty than practical, I think. I prefer the freezer-bag version, which clasps the bottle in a jacket filled with a deep-frozen jelly; the only method I know which is even quicker-acting than an ice bucket.

What do you do if you are caught far from home, without any of these gadgets, dying of thirst and clutching a warm bottle of wine? In many a hotel bathroom I have wrapped the bottle in a wet towel and stood it in the draught of a half-open window. A rudimentary back-of-the-car technique on your way to a picnic is to roll the bottle in a well-soaked newspaper and hold it by an open window – though the police may give you strange looks.

Although it is less often discussed, red wine can be harder to bring to the right temperature than white; 'room temperature' or 'chambré' is the traditional gauge for red wine. But the phrase was coined before the days of central heating. It meant closer to 15·5°C (60°F) than the modern idea of comfort, which is 21°C (70°F) or more. At 21°C or over reds lose their attractive 'cut'. They are no longer refreshing.

Your kitchen is the ideal place to let red wine gradually, over 12 hours or so, reach the perfect temperature. But what if you are in a hurry? Roasting the bottle in front of a fire is a hit-and-miss procedure. I prefer to use the controllable and direct method of a bucket of warm water. Water at 21°C (70°F) will raise the temperature from 13 to 18°C (55 to 65°F) in eight minutes, just as surely as icy water will lower it. If you are decanting the wine, decant it before you warm it.

Meanwhile experiments with microwave ovens continue. I am told that a trained operator can microwave claret to a turn. But having never used one of the devices I leave the question in expert hands.

## Glasses

You would think that a drinking glass, like a corkscrew, would be a simple thing to design. But I never cease to be amazed at the variety of impractical and downright hideous objects that pass for wine glasses. Take the Champagne glass known as a 'coupe', still often used by caterers (it is quicker to fill.) They slander Queen Marie Antoinette by saying that the original was modelled on her breast – the left one, I believe. Whatever the mould may have been, the glass is a horror. You can't avoid spilling from it, the Champagne is flat and all its lovely smell is lost. You want to see the beautiful play of bubbles in Champagne and to have a decent ration that won't spill and leaves room for your nose to have its share of the fun.

Other types that are best avoided include the tinted kind that distort the natural colour of the wine, the pretentious cut-glass thimble, or for my money any cut glass: it is simply too thick. Then there are the 'dock' and 'schooner' that are used for sherry in old-fashioned pubs, glasses with a flaring lip that depend on surface tension even to hold a decent portion – the only way to drink from the horrible things without spilling is to bend double and sip the top off the contents.

Opinions vary about the wide range of glasses designed for specific wines, or even grape varieties – especially by the famous Austrian manufacturer Riedel. There is no doubt

**Above:** *The ideal glass is clear crystal, generous without exaggeration, with a fine, in-curving rim and a substantial foot – all in balance and proportion.*

*These are my own designs for (left to right) sherry, port or Tokay, white wine, Champagne, Grands Crus, red wine, burgundy, a Cognac ballon and snifter.*

about the quality of the company's glasses, whether hand-
or machine-made. Riedel claims that the precise shape of
bowl and rim projects the wine at the part of your mouth that
is most sensitive to a particular attribute of a particular wine.
Hence a glass perfect for a Riesling is not quite right for a
Chardonnay, nor a Cabernet glass for a Pinot Noir – which of
course is no news to the citizens of Bordeaux and Burgundy.
But if wines made from Syrah must have a unique shape of
glass, Sangiovese ditto, and so on, the bill mounts and the
cupboard shrinks ....

I am very much less fussy – or perhaps less discriminating.
I ask only four things of a glass. First, the bowl should be
clear, not coloured, so that I can see what I am drinking.
Second, the glass must be thin enough to allow close sensual
contact between hand and wine, and wine and lip. Third, the
glass must be big enough to hold a proper ration without
being filled to the brim. Third, the top should funnel inward
and not flare out.

The glass used by experts in Bordeaux is close to my
ideal. It holds 17cl (6fl oz) when filled halfway. The shape is
elegant, the balance in your hand is just right. And, above all,
when you hang your nose over the rim you get the full blast
of the expensive aromas you have paid for. The top half of
the glass plays the part of a fume chamber. If you see wine
professionals, growers or merchants swirling the wine
around in their glasses and then inhaling before they taste,
they are not being guilty of a precious mannerism. They are
using the walls of the glass to give the wine the maximum
exposure to the air – thus to volatize its aromatic elements
or, almost literally, to shake out the smell.

Another classic shape is the so-called Paris goblet, a standard piece of equipment in restaurants, and especially marquees, all over the world. Its round belly is not a bad basic shape – if it is big enough. Caterers usually choose the small size and fill it full, thus eliminating any chance of enjoying scent, aroma or bouquet. The big size, filled halfway, would double the pleasure.

Different wine regions have their traditional glass shapes and sizes. A quarter of a litre is reckoned a fair measure of German wine (which admittedly has less alcohol than French). Old German Rhine-wine glasses had thick brown trunks – rather like the Rhinelanders' beloved trees – so that the wine had a reflected amber cast (it made it look older, thus better). But nobody would bang the table with one of the little diamond-cut glasses which the genteel citizens of Trier on the Mosel prefer to show off their equivalently delicate white wines.

The double-spouted Spanish *porón* is another traditional glass, designed so that you can drink from it without it touching your lips. One spout sends a stream of wine directly down your throat while the other lets in air. I strongly suspect that when the Spanish invented this drinking vessel the whole point was to avoid the smell (and as much of the taste as possible). The wine had been kept in goatskins.

The vessel you drink from does affect your appreciation of the wine. So don't use just any old glass. Take a bit of trouble to find the right one. But remain sceptical when anyone suggests that only a huge and very expensive receptacle will do.

# Judging wine

*What it's all about. The moment of truth,
or disenchantment, when you raise the glass.
How to appreciate the look, smell and taste of the
wine. In short, how to savour every
glass to the full.*

Why does a mother hold her child's nose when there is medicine to swallow? The nose is the aerial for the organs of taste in your tongue, palate and throat. Cut off the aerial and you don't get much of a picture. It makes bitter medicine tolerable. But it's a terrible waste of good wine.

*Above: Tipping the glass against a light is one way of examining the wine's colour. A better one, in a good light, is to hold it against white paper.*

Yet isn't this in effect what most wine drinkers do without thinking? Watch them. They give their glass a cursory glance (to make sure there's something in it), then it goes straight to their lips. The configuration of our faces obliges it to pass beneath the nose. But how often do you see it pause there, for the nostrils to register its message? Not often. The art of getting the most from wine is not complicated. But it does have to be learned.

Lesson one is to give it a chance. Any wine that is worth a premium is worth more than a clink and a swallow. How else do you justify the premium?

The art of tasting has been expounded and expanded to fill volumes. Professional tasters stake their names, and large sums, on subtle distinctions that give grounds for investing in a wine's development far into the future. They analyse its character, quality, chemistry, potential and value like a jeweller assessing a stone. But we are talking about enjoyment, not analysis. We start, then, with a straightforward list of wine's distinctive characteristics and pleasures: the points not to be missed.

# Eye

The first is the colour, limpidity, viscosity, brilliance of the wine; its physical presence in the glass. It is the appreciation of the eye. A potent little pool of amber brandy, a glistening cherry tumbler of a young Italian red, the spring-leaf green that tints the pale gold of a glass of Chablis, a sleek ellipsoid of glowing ruby from Bordeaux or the crystal turbulence of Champagne all carry different messages of anticipation. Each is beautiful. Each means something. Each is worth

*Above: Step one in sizing up a wine is simply to look at its appearance in the glass. Hold it up against a white background such as a sheet of paper Tilt the glass away from you so that you can see the colour, clarity and depth of the wine at the rim. With practice this simple trick will enable you to tell a wine's approximate age.*

*Above: Swirling the wine around the glass. This is a way of aerating it so as to release the volatile substances that create the aroma. Shaking the smell out in this way is especially necessary when the wine is low in natural aroma. Any trailing drops falling back down the sides of the glass also give an indication of the wine's texture or viscosity.*

appreciative inspection. Gradations of colour can tell a practised eye the approximate age of a wine – sometimes even its vintage and the variety of its grapes. Each wine has an appropriate colour that experience can teach us to recognize. Cabernet-based wines, for example, are nearly always a deeper, darker red than Pinot Noirs. If it looks pale and thin the odds are that it will taste that way.

Texture, or viscosity, can be equally revealing. Strong wines with concentrated flavours, like blood, are thicker than water. Where such wines wet the sides of the glass (see overleaf) they tend to cling, then, as the alcohol evaporates, fall back in trailing drops that the Germans call 'church-windows'; the British, 'legs', and the romantic, 'tears'.

*Above: Strong and sweet wines tend to stick to the glass, forming 'tears' or 'legs' as they fall back. The explanation is not as simple as it might seem: alcohol adheres to the glass better than water but evaporates more quickly. As it evaporates the wine's water content loses its adhesion and descends. Put your hand over the glass: evaporation stops and so do the 'tears'.*

## Nose

When a professional, a winemaker or merchant, swirls the wine around in his glass before sniffing and sipping he is deliberately aerating the wine as forcefully as possible. Your nose can detect only volatile substances. Some wines are naturally highly aromatic, others less so. The less aromatic it is, the more a taster has to worry the scent out, sniffing for clues like a bloodhound.

The aromas of young wines are essentially the smell of the grapes, transmuted and intensified by fermentation. Unsurprisingly the grapes that make the easiest wines to identify (and at an elementary level, to enjoy) have the most distinctive and memorable smells (aromas is the accepted term) from the moment they become wine. Chardonnay, curiously enough, is not one of these aromatic grapes. It is the people's choice because it makes such a satisfying

**Above:** *Putting the nostrils to work: inhale deeply from the 'fume chamber' of the glass. Much is revealed by the scent of the wine, and the first impression is usually the most telling. Young wine will smell predominantly of the grape from which it was made. Older wines form complex aromas. Much of the pleasure of wine is lost if you skip this stage.*

**Above:** *Assessing the first mouthful. Taste is a combination of what the nostrils have already detected, plus the effect of the alcohol and the non-volatile elements – acids, sugars, tannins and traces of minerals. A generous sip is needed to allow the wine to reach every part of the mouth. Only at this stage can you judge the full 'feel' of the wine.*

mouth- (rather than nose-) full – and because it is commonly seasoned with oak. If new wine is kept in oak barrels the scent of oak overlays and partially conceals the grape smell for a while. (A common short cut is to add oak essence). After the wine is bottled and as it ages the components react and merge. Complex new aromatic substances form. With luck – but not with oak essence – a bouquet is born.

# And mouth

Nose and mouth are not separate organs of sensation. The blocked nose prevents the mouth from tasting. What the nose detects by sniffing, the mouth will confirm by sipping. But only the tongue and palate can reveal the sweetness,

*Above: 'Chewing' the wine to assess its 'body' – the sum of its flavours combined with the warmth and kick of its alcohol. Some tasters draw a little air between their lips and through the wine at this point to help maximize the impression. When you finally swallow, notice what flavour lingers on your palate and in the throat, and for how long.*

*Above: A part of the performance reserved strictly for tasting sessions and not for dinner parties. Spitting out each mouthful, once as much information as possible has been drawn from it, is a way of sampling wines without feeling the effects of the alcohol; perhaps the only fair way to compare a series of wines. Experts develop an accurate aim.*

sourness or bitterness, the fruitiness, the acidity and the tannins, tough or tender, that in their various proportions and interactions make up the taste.

They certainly don't if the wine goes by the vodka route: straight from glass to stomach. Even if it interrupts the conversation, give your wine time to have its say. This means holding it in your mouth for a couple of seconds; for greater effect even chewing it ruminatively. And for maximum effect (but maybe not at dinner) pursing your lips and sucking a thin stream of air through it. The effect of this, while you hold a little wine between your lips and your tongue, is to turn up the volume on the flavour. You may well be surprised how much flavour a mouthful packs if you give it its chance.

Here is a bit of elementary analysis to help you focus on the flavour. Think of it in three stages. The first is the 'attack'. Is it agreeable or aggressive? The second is the 'middle palate' – does it expand on your tongue and satisfy every inquisitive taste-bud? And the third is the 'finish'. What flavour is there left after you have swallowed – and for how long? Poor wines leave either a nasty taste or none at all. Fine wines linger in departing sweetness. And great wines perfume the breath for a full five minutes, maybe more, after each sip.

# The styles of wine

*Silk purses and sows' ears – or what it takes
to make a wine taste the way it does – followed by
eleven basic 'personalities' of wine with a profile of each:
where they are made, how they look and taste, how to
drink them to the best advantage.*

Wine is like Cleopatra; infinite in its variety. There are no two vineyards, cellars or cellarers that ever make an identical wine a second time. There are makers (but they are in a minority) who blend year with year, grape with grape, vineyard with vineyard for consistency. But it is the nature of wine to express more or less clearly the conditions of its making and the state of the raw materials. Add human

*Above: Bordeaux's First Growths are brands as glamorous as those of any couture house. The* chai *of Château Margaux, where its fabulously perfumed* | *wines are kept for their second year in barrel before being bottled, is correspondingly magnificent. The upright barrels are waiting to be filled.*

tastes, skills and fallibility and you have a multitude that no man can number. To try to categorize wine into any sort of pattern is a tall order.

It is often classified or graded for quality, and in a confusing variety of ways. But to index wine's variety of flavour is much harder. The traditional way was by reference to a few 'classical' regions in France, Germany, Spain and Portugal, that supposedly set the styles for everyone to follow. Today, of course, the great majority of the world's wine drinkers have no classical education to fall back on. The current fashion is to take grape variety as the touchstone. But this too has its limitations.

In reality the differences of style that make wine such a rich and rewarding subject are an amalgam of nature and nurture. The better the wine the more its individuality is seen as a prime virtue. Critics argue over the authenticity of a Van Gogh. They can get almost as stressed over the typicity of a Château Margaux.

## Prime factors

What makes one wine different from another? In order of importance the prime influences are: (1) the intentions and skill of the winemaker, (2) the grape variety, (3) the climate, (4) the weather, (5) the character of the soil, (6) how old or young the wine is.

The winemaker is almost always working within a tradition or convention, rather than trying to introduce a brand new brew to the world – though this does happen from time to time. Certainly in Europe he or she is also working within a pretty strict set of rules; wine laws of a kind

*Left: Cabernet Sauvignon was introduced in Bordeaux 200 years ago as an improvement on the Cabernet Franc and Malbec which then dominated the vineyards. (It may be a cross between Cabernet Franc and Sauvignon Blanc.) Today it is the world's most prestigious red grape, giving its deep colour, fragrance and tannic structure to wines from every wine country and region with the warmth to ripen it.*

that don't exist in the newer wine-growing countries. So the most important factor is the success or failure of his efforts, starting in the vineyard and continuing in the cellar. Of these two the vineyard is the more important: you can make bad wine from good grapes, but nobody can make good wine from bad grapes.

Factor two, the grape variety, is nowadays often seen as the thing that matters most. Most people know that red and rosé wine are made of red grapes and that white wine is usually made of white grapes (to make white wine out of red grapes is an expensive eccentricity practised only when the price is right – for example in Champagne). But beyond such basic facts nobody, until relatively recently, seemed to know or care which grapes were used. At any rate they didn't talk about it.

Over the past 30 years or so all that has changed. California, Australia and the rest of the new wine world, from Chile to New Zealand, take the variety as their starting point.

When the New World stopped calling any of its good reds burgundy and started specifying which one was made of Pinot Noir, attention was suddenly focused for the first time on the basic taste and smell of the raw material; the grape. 'varietal character' became a catch-phrase.

The point rapidly sank in that the sows' ears that won't make silk purses include most of the world's standard bulk-producing grape varieties. Only a score or so of 'noble' grapes are capable of producing good 'varietal' wine.

Factor three, the climate, matters less than it did. It used to be crucial. It decided how ripe the grapes were at picking time, and once picked how fast they fermented. Very ripe grapes, fermented very fast, made characterless wine. But along came refrigeration and with it the means of almost

*Above: Climate, and even more vineyard slope and exposure, are most important in marginal wine regions. On the River Mosel in Germany only south-facing slopes will ripen the classic Riesling grape. Less well-placed sites are planted with inferior crosses such as Müller-Thurgau.*

total control. Winemakers discovered how to pick at the ideal moment and keep the juice cool. The result: fine fragrant wines from hot climates – a drastic narrowing of the gap between the old fine-wine belt, where vintage time is cool, and the former bulk-wine belt, where it is hot.

Factor four, the weather, used to be decisive. It can still be. Serious frost, hail or rain at the wrong moment can wipe out a harvest. But the daily vagaries of temperature and humidity have less drastic effects than they used to, as grape-growers master techniques of pruning and training their vines, and spraying and draining their vineyards to get the best out of even the worst seasons.

As for soil, factor five, a Frenchman will tell you it matters most of all. But then the *terroir* he is defending is his birthright. Some Australians will tell you a vine can grow good grapes almost anywhere. (But then that is just where he has

**Above:** *Vineyard soils range from this broken slate (on the Mosel) to chalk (in Champagne) to gravel (Médoc and Graves) to clay (Chablis) to sandstone.*

*Some say only the soil temperature and drainage matter. There must be more intimate links with wine quality and flavour, but they have yet to be proven.*

planted it.) Soil does matter, especially from the point of view of drainage. Its physical structure is more important than its chemistry. But any direct link between soil and wine quality is hard to prove, and with wine style even harder.

## When age is an advantage

The sixth factor cuts across and qualifies the first five. It is age. Far from being an automatic plus, age rapidly becomes a threat to the great majority of wines. They should really be sold with a 'Drink before ...' date like milk. One year is a good age for most white wines, and up to two years for the great ocean of simple reds.

The only wines that need to be stored away before opening are those with concentrated flavour which are harsh with tannins or acidity at first, but which experience has taught will develop smoothness and complex flavours with age.

The price, if no other clues are available, will usually tell you which they are. It stands to reason that few, if any, short-lived 'drink by ...' wines are likely to change hands for much money. The blue-chip wines are all those that have a storage life of at least five or maybe up to 50 years, with the certainty or high probability that somewhere along the line between awkward youth and feeble old age, they will be marvellously satisfying to drink, with dimensions, depths, nuances of flavour that no unaged wine can ever achieve.

## Eleven basic modes

The following, then, are 11 broadly defined styles of wine, the results of differing combinations of our six factors, with typical examples of and suitable uses for each.

## Dry white wines with a simple flavour and without very distinct aromas

Wines made from grapes with no readily identifiable aroma form the bulk of this category. They are the equivalent of background music – agreeable, but not a concert performance demanding your attention. Youth and freshness are essential: these wines get tired quickly. They are often drunk as aperitifs, but can rapidly become boring without the addition of another flavour. Blackcurrant juice (*cassis*) is a favourite. With soda or sparkling mineral water they make a 'spritzer'. As partners to food they have almost limitless uses, rarely rising to gastronomic heights but always helping the appetite along with fish, cold meats, sausages, terrines, strongly garlicky dishes or curries which would smother fine wines. Serve them a few degrees colder than better or more delicate whites.

Most branded dry whites, jug or carafe wines fit into this category. They are usually made in large quantities in a warm climate – the San Joaquin Valley of California, for example. The leaders of this group, those with names and histories, include Entre-Deux-Mers and other simple white Bordeaux, Muscadet, supermarket-level Chablis, Gaillac, most Sylvaner and Pinot Blanc from Alsace, Aligoté from Burgundy and everyday Mâcon Blanc. Italy's Soave, Verdicchio, Frascati, Pinot Bianco, Vermentino, Malvasia, Trebbiano, Orvieto Secco and Sicilian whites usually belong in this category; Italian taste in white wines is peculiarly neutral, as though the taste and smell of grapes gave offence. California's cheaper whites nearly all belong here,

whether called 'Chablis', Chenin Blanc, Mountain White or
whatever. Australia's cheap 'cask' wines tend to belong in
the next, more perfumed, category. The first of them to
make a hit was bizarrely labelled 'Moselle'. Most Spanish
whites belong here. Portuguese *vinho verde* is a light and
fizzy version. Switzerland's Fendant and Johannisberg can
be remarkably potent and convincing examples.

It is a wide spectrum without dramatic extremes –
essential as a foundation for more exotic wine-drinking.

## Lightweight aromatic whites with grapey flavours and more or less fruity/flowery scents

Germany provides the models for this
category. German wines are low in alcohol
and correspondingly 'transparent' in flavour.
The object is the scented crispness of fresh fruit, either
balanced with a degree of sweetness or in the fashionable (at
least in Germany) *Trocken*, sugar-free style.

At the bottom end of the quality scale (for example
Liebfraumilch or Niersteiner Domtal) they can be dismal
potations; water and sugar their principal flavours. But at the
top they can be the most exquisite of all wines for solo
sipping. Their true role is to be drunk on their own. Use
them for wine parties, as aperitifs, while reading or writing
letters or watching television – any time when refreshment
and fragrance are more important than flavour and alcohol.
In summer they are perfect garden wines, thoroughly chilled.
In winter I like an after-dinner glass just pleasantly cool.
Good-quality German estate wines, whether from the Rhine

or the Mosel, are the epitome of this class, and the Riesling is the model grape. The stepping stones from delicate to rich are Kabinett, Spätlese, Auslese. Ausleses were formerly all sweet; today they are frequently fully fermented to become dry – and very potent.

France's aromatic answers are Rieslings and Gewürztraminers from Alsace (which are weightier in body and alcohol and usually drier) and Sauvignon Blancs from the Loire (Touraine), the Dordogne, parts of the south-west and even the Midi. Colombard is a minor player here too. Austrian Grüner Veltliner in its first year can be one of the most thrilling and convincing examples of this most appetizing style. The Italian Tirol and Friuli and adjacent Slovenia also excel here. So does Australia with its exceptionally tasty Rieslings. New Zealand uses Riesling, Gewürztraminer and sometimes Chenin Blanc to go for the same effect. England is doing better every year, mainly with Müller-Thurgau and such new German varieties as Huxelrebe and Reichensteiner – which many find just too aromatic. California's freshest Gewürztraminers and Rieslings are sometimes in this style, but more often full-bodied; very much wines for tasty food. Argentina's Torrontes is outrageously perfumed; hard to match with anything.

## Sparkling wines, with Champagne as the boss

There is an enormous range of quality and style between a plain white wine with bubbles and the sinful opulence of the silkiest Champagne. Scarcely a wine region in the

*Above: The 'elaboration' of Champagne involves more manual work than any other wine. The crucial step is to persuade dead yeast cells from the second fermentation (which produces the fizz) to rest on the cork so that they can be extracted. Here in the Roederer cellars a remueur 'riddles' bottles of Crystal.*

world has not made its bid recently to enter this huge growth area. The best non-Champagne sparkling wines come from Burgundy (Crémant de Bourgogne), the Loire (Crémant de la Loire), Alsace (Crémant d'Alsace), south-west France (Blanquette de Limoux), Catalonia (top *cava* wines from such firms as Codorníu and Freixenet), northern Italy (Lombardy, Trentino, Piedmont), Germany (high-grade *Sekt*), California – where several French Champagne firms have established cellars – Australia and New Zealand. The cooler zones of Australia and New Zealand's Marlborough are the places that should cause most alarm back in Champagne.

All use the Champagne method (*méthode champenoise*) and used to proclaim it on their labels. Jealously, the French now restrict them to 'classic method', in whatever language. Other sparkling wines, even Russian Champanski, can be fun, but are usually more so flavoured with fresh orange juice or a drop of syrup (blackcurrant, grenadine or strawberry). The ultimate 'fun' wines are sweet sparkling muscats, of very low alcoholic strength but honey sweetness, with Asti Spumante at their head.

### Assertive, full-bodied dry whites with positive characters derived from the best grapes and/or maturity

White burgundy, the marriage of Chardonnay grapes and small oak barrels, is the epitome of this class. But all France's best dry whites have the same profile: relatively discreet aromas, mouth-filling flavour and firm structure, generous alcohol (about 13 degrees) giving appetizing succulence without distinct sweetness. Their aim and purpose is to accompany food. They are fatiguing to drink without it. Their flavour is as strong as that of most red wines; don't lose it by over-chilling.

The list starts with the Chardonnay grape almost everywhere it is grown. It needs at least a year in bottle, usually two or more, to reach its full flavour. High-quality mature wines from the following grapes and areas can be bracketed here as the best meal-time whites, with almost any savoury food: Chardonnay, Riesling, Sauvignon Blanc, Gewürztraminer, Pinot Gris, Chenin Blanc, Sémillon, Marsanne, Viognier, Malvasia, Grechetto, Furmint (all these

are grapes) from Burgundy, Alsace, Graves, the Upper Loire
(Sancerre and Pouilly), Anjou (Savennières), the northern
Rhône, Catalonia, Italy, Austria, Hungary, Slovenia, Bulgaria,
coastal California, Australia, South Africa, Chile, Argentina
and New Zealand. Also the best white Riojas and classic
examples of Frascati, Soave, Orvieto Secco, Pinot Grigio
(especially from Collio), and so on. Montilla and manzanilla
finos from Andalucía can be included, and so can the old-
fashioned characters of Austro-Hungary: Szürkebaràt,
Rotgipfler, Ruländer – if you can find them.

### Sweet white wines

These, like sweet dishes, come at the end of
most people's meal-plan. Not all, though; the
Bordeaux idea of heaven is not caviar to the
sound of trumpets, but foie gras to the sip of
Sauternes – a sublime marriage of the
sweetest wine with the richest food.

Oddly, where most wines taste best with food of
comparable or not dissimilar flavour, sweet wines show to
their best advantage with contrasting food, or no food at all.
However good a Sauternes may be, it doesn't add much to a
beautiful apple tart, all butter and caramelized fruit. But it
illuminates a savoury foie gras and faces up to strong and
salty cheeses as no red wine can.

Sauternes (and its colleague Barsac) is the champion
of sweet table wines, leading a fairly limited field. The other
runners are 'liquorous' (sticky and golden) wines from the
neighbouring Bordeaux villages of Ste-Croix-du-Mont,
Loupiac and Cérons, Monbazillac from the Dordogne not

far away, and *moelleux* Loire wines made in rare autumns in
Anjou (Bonnezeaux, Quarts de Chaume, Coteaux du Layon)
and Vouvray. Alsace makes outstandingly high-flavoured
late-picked Rieslings and Gewürztraminers that can be used
in the same way. So does Austria with its Ausbruch and
Beerenauslese wines from the Burgenland, and likewise
Hungary since the recent renaissance of its fabled Tokay.
All these are powerfully flavoured and all (except Tokay)
fairly high in alcohol.

In contrast the fabulously rare, very sweet wines of
Germany, top Ausleses, Beerenausleses and
Trockenbeerenausleses, are low in alcohol and, like their
drier counterparts, are unquestionably best sipped after or
between meals.

Perhaps the most aromatic of all sweet wines are made of
Muscat grapes, in all degrees of sweetness and strength
ranging from an almost treacly character (as in the five-star
brown liqueur muscats of north-east Victoria, Australia) to
wines that are so delicate that they have to be kept under
refrigeration – a speciality of one or two Napa Valley growers.
The lower Rhône Valley and delta produce some admirable
sweet-but-not-heavy muscats, led by Beaumes-de-Venise
and Frontignan. Roussillon and Rivesaltes in the extreme
south of France make stronger wines. Sicily, Portugal
(Setúbal) and the Crimea all make delicious brown muscats,
but without ever really putting them on the map.

The world used to drink much more sweet wine than it
does today – though there are signs that sweet-lovers are
gaining confidence, at last giving themselves permission to
indulge. Isolated examples of excellent indulgences crop up

in Cyprus (Commandaria), France (Banyuls), Tarragona (Priorato Dulce and Pajarete), Malaga, Marsala and in California's rare but potentially sublime Angelica.

### Rosé wines, from camisole pink to onion-skin orange

There is no prestige in being a middle-of-the-roader, but you collect a lot of friends. Pink wines are made as though they were going to be red until the winemaker suddenly changed his mind. He makes a white wine of red grapes, stained with their skins but not toughened with their tannins. If the grapes are aromatic, the rosé can be fabulously so. Burgundy's one rosé, Marsannay, can smell more ravishingly of new-born Pinot Noir than any wine. Cabernet Sauvignon makes excellent rosé in California and Cabernet Franc in Anjou. Grenache, a sweet but unscented grape, makes strong but unscented rosé. Tavel, the one famous example, always strikes me as making the best of a bad job.

Broadly, you can divide rosé into pink-with-a-hint-of-blue (var. camisole) and pink-with-more-than-a-hint-of-brown (var. onion skin). Anjou typifies the first, Tavel the second. Wines that are just off-white, the palest of pinks, as though by mistake, are called by the French '*vins gris*' – grey wines – and by the Californians (who do it with Zinfandel) 'blush'.

Champagne, made with Pinot Noir, used not infrequently to be faintly grey. But pink Champagne today is stained a clear, bright pink by adding a dose of the region's red. It is one of the prettiest and most luxurious of all wines.

## Fresh grapey young reds

Beaujolais is the first name in a class of wine whose star seems, for the moment, to be waning. If the most 'serious' white wines invade red territory with their savoury richness, these lighthearted reds cross the (anyway vague) border into a class of flavour associated with white wine. Like whites they rely on acidity for their bite and liveliness (reds have acidity too, but back it up with tannin). In the conventional ordering of several wines, red comes after white. You can treat these wines as young whites – and serve them almost as cool. Above all don't try to age them more than a few months: the bottom falls out. Without their simple childlike vitality they are dull and thin. Drink them young, with food (any food except highly savoury gamey dishes) or without. They go as well as white wine (and often better than mature red) with cheese.

Any wine sold as 'Nouveau', 'Primeur' or 'Novello' should be in this style. Simple young red Bordeaux should be, too. And if young Midi or Rhône wine is like this you have hit a good one. The lively Cabernet reds of Anjou and Touraine are often of this character – growing redder and more serious only in warm vintages. The best of France's many *vins de pays* qualify in the same way. Italy offers Valpolicella, Bardolino and Chiaretto in this style, and sometimes a vivid Dolcetto from Piedmont, too. Lambrusco, traditionally at least, is this kind of wine with more bubbles; Chianti, with less.

Spain and Portugal make grapey young reds only on their Atlantic coast. Few people know that the bulk of Portugal's *vinho verde* is red; tourists find it a bit rough and ready.

Sadly this sort of essentially frivolous fresh and lively red is not the goal of many wine-makers in California, Australia, South America and South Africa.

*Above: The* fiasco *of Chianti used to be the symbol of good cheer in all Italian restaurants. But the deliciously lively drink of the Tuscan farmer, often slightly* sweet and fizzy, is a prime example of wine that 'won't travel'. Outside Tuscany, you are wiser to choose Chianti Classico aged in a Bordeaux-style bottle.

## Standard low-price reds, whether sold in jug, bag or bottle

This was once the most popular of all classes of wine, as France's *vin ordinaire*, blended to be just sufficiently tasty, reasonably smooth, moderately alcoholic, and a decent shade of red. What it misses is charm, vitality and individuality. French versions tend to be dry, thin and watery; Italian, South American and Californian distinctly sweeter, and Spanish softer and stronger. Any pretension in serving them (unless as a joke) is absurd. To a Frenchman or an Italian they were traditionally (before he bought a car) like the Englishman's cup of tea – always on tap. For refreshment's sake they are drunk on the cool side.

It is worth noting that the official EEC category of 'table wine', which covers this no-pretensions department, also covers any wine made outside the framework of national denominations. It is one of the many follies of bureaucracy that, for example, several of Italy's most distinguished wines, made with justified scorn for the official DOC system, are ranked in EEC language as '*vino de tavola*'.

### Medium- to full-bodied reds made for maturing

A pretty dull definition of the majority of the greatest red wines: red Bordeaux and burgundy, Rhônes and Riojas, the finest Cabernets, Pinot Noirs and Zinfandels of California, their equivalents from the Pacific Northwest and Australia, top Chianti Classicos and such originals as Sassicaia and Tignanello, Torgiano and Carmignano. Portugal enters its best garrafeiras from Dão, Douro, the Alentejo and Bairrada, Spain the cream of Penedès, Duero and Navarra reds, Chile, South Africa and New Zealand their fast-improving Cabernets and Merlots. Their common characteristic (though less so with the majority of New World wines) is that they need time, in barrel and bottle, to fulfil their potential. To drink a fine Bordeaux or burgundy before it is at least five years old is to forgo the quality you

*Left: Justified excitement about the wines of the 'New World' often forgets that modern Italian wine fits this description too. Almost everything has changed since the days of the old local wine-shops. From the Alps to the heel of Italy, modern concepts of wine-making now produce scores of clean, stable, full-bodied reds of real local character but international appeal. The same is not true, alas, of whites.*

paid a premium for. Long vatting plumps them up with tannins, pigments and all manner of tasty stuff. Time moulds these elements into what has been called 'a chemical symphony'. Harmony between the component flavours is what you are waiting for. The dark deposit you often find in wines of this class is the fall-out from these changes.

Don't overwhelm their flavours with the strongest-tasting dishes. Roast meats are excellent, poultry, too, but not well-hung game or any highly seasoned food. Beware also of cheese. Only the milder cheeses consort well with fine mature red wines.

### The darkest, most full-blooded, turbo-powered reds

Mediterranean regions, given the chance, will ripen red grapes to sticky blackness almost every year. In northern Europe it takes an exceptional summer. The result, in either case, is a darker, more potent wine than the normal

Bordeaux or burgundy. California's Napa Valley made its name with this type of wine. Most of the growers are now aiming for something more subtle. Châteauneuf-du-Pape and Hermitage, Bandol, Barolo, Barbaresco, Brunello di Montalcino, Vega Sicilia in Spain, Australia's massively succulent Barossa Shiraz are classics of the genre.

The rare vintages of Bordeaux that reach this degree of concentration have included 1945, '61, '82 and '90. Burgundy scarcely ever makes this kind of wine.

Black and daunting as these wines may be they can be a memorable experience drunk young: tannic and sweet with concentrated fruit at the same time. In youth they can even match powerful cheeses. But mature, with their colour ebbing and an autumnal smell coming on, they enter another realm of voluptuous sensations.

## Wines with added alcohol

'Fortified' or 'dessert' wines – port, sherry, Madeira and their look-alikes – have only one thing in common: they have been topped up with alcohol (brandy or another spirit) to make them stronger. Port is brandied to keep it sweet, sherry to keep it stable. Fortified wines can improve with age for improbable periods. But don't be misled into thinking this includes time decorating the sideboard in a decanter. Like all other wines they fade if left for long in contact with the air.

# Wine with meals

*Mating and matching, contrasting and complementing. Why port goes with Stilton and claret with wild strawberries. The challenging and often controversial business of putting wine and food together in the ideal combination.*

White with fish, red with meat is not a law, like driving on the left when you land at Dover. You are not going to hit anyone coming the other way. But you have to start somewhere. Clichés can be useful.

I have always been guilty of choosing wines for people rather than for dishes. When on my own I drink what I feel like drinking. No, it isn't always Champagne. When it's a twosome, I find out (if I don't know already) what sort of wine my friend enjoys and open a bottle. When it's a larger party, a combination of the company, occasion, mood and domestic economy usually narrows the field enough to make choosing fairly easy. Occasion? Is it a family meal, a business lunch or an evening celebration? Mood? Do I feel lavish, experimental, or do I want to play it safe? Economy? I feel happier ordering something I can easily afford (especially in restaurants) than going for a mortgage, so to speak.

My attitude to wine comes with seeing it as a social drink rather than a condiment for food. Committed foodies may be scandalized, but I find the times are rare when my choice of wine is guided – rather than simply influenced – by the precise flavours of a dish.

# The art of matchmaking

An impressionistic approach gets you close enough. You have learned by experience what flavour to expect in, say, lamb or liver. With experience you learn approximately what weight and aroma to expect from, say, a fresh Beaujolais, a five-year-old Pomerol or a two-year-old Sonoma Chardonnay.

The art of matching wine with food consists of a moment's imagination – a mental scanning of the two repertoires. Think of them, if you like, as two colour wheels. You can turn them until you find a close match, or a total contrast, or some pleasing combination in between.

The catch is that you need enough experience of different wines to colour your own wheel. Few people ever seem to get this far (and winemakers almost never: in Burgundy all they know is what food tastes good with burgundy).

The categories of wine outlined in the last chapter are a start, at least, at devising a wine-wheel. It would be foolhardy to be categorical in the same way about food. Rather than make a long mouth-watering list of every dish, bland and spicy, that I can think of; let us see what we mean by contrasting flavours, and what matching them involves.

Contrast (or complement) is epitomized by the appalling British habit of dousing fatty food with vinegary sauces. French fried potatoes with tomato ketchup and jellied eels with vinegar like battery acid are a couple of gross examples. A rather more delicate one is Chablis with shellfish. Crab and lobster meat is rich, dense and quite detectably sweet. The clean, slightly tart, mineral flavour of Chablis whets the appetite for more. A quite different sort of contrast between food and wine is found in the German taste for pairing pungent, well-hung game, venison or wild boar, with a sweet and velvety Riesling Auslese.

Sancerre on the Loire is known for two famous products: its aromatic dry white wine and its salty, crumbly, powerfully goaty cheese. The two are admirably complementary. Sancerre may be a light wine compared with, say, a red burgundy or a red Rhône, but its acidity and aromas fight back at the cheese in an ideal pairing, where a fleshy red wine would be helplessly pinned to the ropes.

The extreme saltiness of real French Roquefort is already in contrast with its luxurious buttery texture. Add the sweetness of Sauternes to the richness of the cream and its bite is diminished to agreeable piquancy. The English follow the same principle in drinking fruity port with their highly savoury Stilton.

Closely paired flavours are commoner in practice than complementary ones. Take a couple of examples much favoured in Bordeaux: fragrant flesh of lamb from the riverside marshes with an almost herbal Médoc, or the fat

*Left: Port and Stilton is one of the remarkably few traditional wine-and-food pairings that really works. Contrary to accepted wisdom, most cheese is the enemy of most red wine. Note the solecism in the picture: some evil-intentioned person has scooped a cavity in the cheese, apparently to fill it with port. The result will be a disgusting mush. Stilton should always be cut; never 'scooped'.*

*Left: Fresh foie gras was once the ultimate rarity; today it seems all parts of France and much of central Europe make it. It is a killer of red wines and dry whites taste scrawny with it. The perfect match is Sauternes, Monbazillac from the Dordogne or a Basque Jurançon* moelleux *– or the ancestor of Sauternes, Hungarian Tokaji Aszú.*

lampreys of the Dordogne stewed in strong St-Emilion and served with the same wine on the table. Here the citizens of Bordeaux are matching food and wine in close harmony. Their apparently eccentric choice of Sauternes with dangerously rich foie gras follows the same logic. Even their habit of pouring old claret over wild wood strawberries, in place of cream, is designed to bring out a hint of strawberry in the wine, and no doubt vice versa – you have to taste this combination to believe it.

## Problem pairings

There is a handful of flavours that never seem to work with wine. Oily smoked fish, such as smoked salmon, is difficult to match, but try fino sherry with it. There is a salty authority in the wine that emphasises the rich flavour of the salmon. Asparagus is not easy either; Sauvignon Blancs seem to echo the flavour, fat Chardonnays meet it head on; curiously enough such sweet wines as late-harvest Alsace give it zest.

Chocolate is the most notorious: neither pairing nor contrasting really seems to work. The most successful wines, for a reason I don't fully understand, seem to be Madeira and

Tokay. What they have in common is sweetness with a high level of acidity. Citrus fruit is very tricky. You can drink sweet wines with, say, caramelized oranges, but the wine almost disappears.

Sweet dishes in general tend to come off better than any sweet wines chosen to partner them. To me Tokay works best of all – but when I say that it is only right that I declare a business interest (I helped to found a company to resurrect Tokay after the calamities of communism).

To taste port or Madeira or old Sauternes at their best try the contrast of a plain sponge cake, or a plate of filberts. In the same way there are whole cultures of cookery that are, at least on the face of it, inimical to wine. Oriental food, whether Indian, Chinese, Japanese or any other, relies on seasonings that threaten to smother the taste of wine. Nobody knows for sure whether the almost total absence of wine in the ancient cultures of the East was due to the native seasonings or the physique of the inhabitants or both. But we are all finding out that it is not, after all, a gastronomic mismatch without hope. Experiment leads to unexpected harmonies; all that is needed is an open mind. Châteauneuf-du-Pape with curry, dry sherry (whether fino or oloroso) with sushi, red burgundy with shabu shabu, Riesling with Cantonese seafood, can all ring bells. If one Asian cuisine has (so far) found me at a loss it is lemon-grass-smothered Thai food.

Just as food can smother the flavour of wine, so can another wine that is more full-bodied or flavoursome. Tradition has handed down to us a commonsensical order of play in which light wines come before weightier ones. This is often interpreted to mean that all (dry) whites should precede all red. But as the categories suggested in the previous chapter show, there are light reds and weighty whites. Let the volume of flavour, not the colour, be the guide.

Convention also decrees that in a meal with two similar wines – say two red Bordeaux of about the same quality but different ages – the younger should be served before the older. This is despite the fact that the older may be more faded and, in reality, lighter. There is good sense in the tradition: the more complex flavours of the older wine would make the younger taste simplistic and two-dimensional if it were served after.

In practice I often prefer to serve the two similar wines side by side, or in quite rapid succession, so that friends can enjoy comparing and contrasting.

*Above:* No wine has such a complete gamut of styles as the glorious range offered by sherry – from (right to left) delicate dry fino, mature and nutty fino amontillado, vigorous dry amontillado, resounding dry oloroso – one of the most piquant and penetrating wines – to luscious, liqueur-like Pedro Ximénez.

# Special occasions

*Parties and picnics, barbecues and beanfeasts,*
*functions and fireside tête-à-têtes ... how to choose a*
*wine to do justice to the occasion, and how to make*
*sure that you don't run out.*

I s there is such a thing as the 'correct' wine for a particular
occasion? Maybe Champagne is de rigueur for race
meetings and society weddings. But in general appropriateness
is purely subjective. There is an occasion for every wine, but
many possible wines for any occasion. These are my thoughts
on accommodating as many of the treats on offer as possible
in a convivial life.

**Above:** *Different social events can have*
*their own drinking traditions. While*
*horse-racing and Champagne will always*
*be closely linked, the annual regatta at*

*Henley-on-Thames has a traditional*
*liaison with Pimm's No.1, that insidious*
*brew of unpredictable potency. Or*
*Champagne for those who insist.*

# Wine before meals

A clever fellow (it must have been in the 1970s) coined the phrase 'the thinking man's martini'. He was talking about Chardonnay. A glass of white wine, the implication goes, is not a 'drink' in the drinking man's sense. But it is. I don't know how deep your martinis are, but five ounces – a decent glass – of French or California (not German) white wine are exactly as strong as one and a half of gin – the normal barman's measure. In terms of pure alcohol, a drink is a drink, whether it be wine, whisky or indeed beer. The differences between drinks and their effects have more to do with factors such as timing (how quickly you swallow a given dose) and, of course, alcoholic content. Most important of all is whether a drink is combined with food.

Wine is the 'drink of moderation'. Why? Not because it is weaker, but because it belongs with food. To introduce a note of sombre realism, road casualty figures paint the picture very clearly. Long-term research in New Zealand has shown that drink-related accidents are rarely caused by people who have wined and dined. Wined without dining, yes, but more often beered or whiskied without dining.

It is the food that makes the difference. This is partly, perhaps mainly, because it 'lines the stomach' and slows the ingestion of alcohol into the bloodstream. But equally important is the fact that when we drink wine and eat at the same time, or sip and nibble, we take in alcohol at a more leisurely pace. If you quench thirst without satisfying hunger, more drink becomes a substitute for the food you need. You quell hunger pangs by drinking more – an almost certain way of taking more alcohol more quickly than you intend.

Wine can be the perfect appetizer. For me Champagne beats all other aperitifs by several lengths, with only fino sherry in the same furlong. But it is no more a 'safe' drink than any other if you swallow glass after glass without accompanying food. Canapés, bread, nuts or crisps are the minimum. Better still, avoid the overlong 'cocktail' session (often caused by late-arriving guests) and sit down promptly to drink your wine (and some water, too) as an appetizing and satisfying part of a leisurely meal.

Which are the best aperitif wines? Anything with a distinct flavour, but not over-emphatic, fruity, heavy, oaky or astringent. To me freshness and lightness are prime qualities in an aperitif, so long as there is a definite enough flavour. Good-quality German wines are often perfect to drink before a meal: strong on aroma and with a nice acidic 'cut' that whets the appetite, but relatively low in alcohol. Poor-quality German 'Tafelwein', in contrast, lacks every aperitif quality. It is watery, insipid, vaguely sweet ... no thank you.

What makes Champagne (or another sparkling wine) so ideal? The answer is its powerful flavour, the result of prolonged fermentation, combined with the 'lift', the zing that the bubbles give it. Champagne has about the same alcohol content as other French white wines, but its alcohol becomes effective more quickly because the dissolved carbon dioxide in the wine goes straight into your bloodstream. Your circulation reacts by speeding up, just as it does when you are running, to exchange carbon dioxide for oxygen. So a faster bloodstream carries the alcohol around your system. You giggle sooner, but the effects pass off more rapidly.

**Above:** *No Spaniard would be so thoughtless as to drink without food. Tapas, which can range from a bowl of olives to a minor feast of prawns,* squid, sausages, steak and cheese, stand on every bar to accompany the chilled fino sherry. The standard ration is half a bottle a head.

Freshness and lightness, I'll admit, are not everyone's cup of tea. Some people find natural wines insipid on their own. They want more of the feel of alcohol, the warmth that their dosing with spirits give to sherry, port or vermouth. The French reveal an unexpectedly sweet tooth by enjoying port as an aperitif. The Italians evince their craving for bitterness by their wormwood concoctions, their Camparis and Carpanos.

In Spain, and in the Anglo-Saxon countries too, fino sherry is generally agreed to be the finest of aperitifs. Its delicately dry, distinctly savoury, sometimes almost salty flavour does not so much suggest as demand the savoury miniature dishes, the tapas, that every Spanish bar so wisely and profitably provides.

# Wine after meals

Convention shapes our taste. The Japanese day begins with pickled fish, soup and a bowl of rice. The Western dinner ends with sweet wines. We can rationalize it by saying that sugar sates appetite, so (being affluent) we keep it until the last. But the Japanese say the same about rice.

Convention, then, gives us a list of possible end-of-dinner wines. It starts with port, reminds us of Madeira, curtsies to history by including Marsala and Malaga, then passes to Sauternes and all the gold-to-amber products of 'nobly rotten' grapes: Auslese from Germany, Ausbruchs from Austria, late-harvest wines from California, Alsace, Australia, *moelleux* from the Loire Valley, decadent butterscotch Tokay. Under a separate rubric it lists all the world's aromatic muscat wines, from fruity and sparkling Asti Spumante to

Australia's unique liqueur version, like chocolate velvet.
France's fashionable (and economical) entry is Muscat de
Beaumes-de-Venise. They are all good in their way. There is
only one conventionally accepted dessert wine which I,
personally, can find no use for, and that is sweet Champagne.
Even bottles labelled 'Rich' are never sweet enough for their
intended use. I take issue with French taste here as I do over
their taste for port as an aperitif. Champagne and desserts
should be kept apart.

Are these sweet wines meant to partner food, or to drink
on their own? They can work well either way. It is not always
easy to match two sweet tastes successfully: one must be
allowed to dominate. If the dessert does, the wine might as
well be sugared water. A good dish for a sweet wine should
be a simple, and not a very sugary, one. The stress should be
on richness rather than sweetness. A plain fruit tart with
buttery pastry gives any sweet wine a perfect background: a
lemon meringue pie can only fight the wine, and will
probably win.

In such cases the logical procedure is to eat the dessert
first, sip a glass of water, and then enjoy the wine.

Separated from a direct match with sweet food, the list of
possible choices goes far beyond the conventional. Any wine
you drink after eating needs to be good. It needs more
substance or flavour than it could get away with before the
meal. This said, almost anything goes. A mature bottle of red
wine, a glass of tawny port or a fine refreshing Riesling can
be equally satisfying.

And after the meal is a good time to celebrate with a
bottle of (Brut) Champagne.

# When a little goes a long way

Logic tells you that the better a wine is the more of it you will want to drink. Indeed my own wine-judging system (these days everyone has to have one) is based purely on desirability. The lowest possible score is one sniff: "No thank you". One sip is almost equally dismissive, two faintly exploratory; one glass pretty damning, two either curious or desperate .... It becomes more telling when we reach the two-bottle level. If you want a second bottle it says something pretty positive about the first.

Yet doing the sums as a host preparing a party I find the First Law of Oenoconomy points in another direction. Give guests wine with the sort of concentrated character they can't miss and they will actually swallow less of it. Good wine satisfies with each sip. In terms of flavour per unit of volume, great wine beats ordinary wine by a factor of, I would say, about ten to one – both in the strength of the flavour and, even more importantly, in its length in your mouth. This means each sip need be only one-tenth the size to make the same impression. Allow for the fact that the impression is delicious, and you want, shall we say, five times as much of it, you still need only half as much volume. Translated into bottles, this means that one bottle of truly fine wine will go as far as two of plonk. No wonder they sell it in gallon jugs.

The French have a measure for the all-important factor of length of flavour – the time the taste persists after you have swallowed the wine. They call it a *caudalie*. One *caudalie* (from the Latin *cauda*, meaning a tail) equals one full second of lingering flavour. If you take a stopwatch to, say, a plain Bordeaux rouge and a (mature) First Growth you will see that the Bordeaux rouge clocks up between one and two seconds before its taste disappears, while the Mouton-Rothschild perfumes your breath for ten, 12, even 20 or more seconds. It is not only scarcity value, but mathematical logic that sets the price of Mouton ten times or more above that of its humble rival.

How, then, do you calculate how much wine you are going to need for a given occasion? A rough rule of thumb, used in manuals for caterers, is that you need an average of one and a half glasses of an aperitif per person, followed by two glasses of wine with a meal, and possibly one more after the meal. A 75-centilitre (24fl oz) wine bottle gives six four-ounce portions. If the aperitif, the table wine and after-dinner wine are all of 'normal' strength the total consumption is, therefore, four and a half glasses or three-quarters of a bottle a head.

If you serve two or three different wines with the meal, the probability is that guests will drink an extra glass, bringing their total consumption up to nearly a bottle each. Spread over the whole length of an evening this is not an excessive amount. Since an average person metabolizes about one 'unit' (or glass) of alcohol per hour, in theory this means that six glasses spread over three hours leaves you with only three units in your system. It is still not a subject I am anxious to discuss with a magistrate.

Whatever caterers' manuals say, there is another phenomenon to be observed: the more people there are in a party the more each person is likely to drink. When you are on your own half a bottle seems enough wine, but when there are two of you one bottle scarcely seems enough.

***Above:*** *Perfect unselfconscious integration of wine and food is achieved in France at a family's Sunday lunch in the garden: a time when the pleasures of the table reach their peak. Even French children, table-trained as they are, get down to play when the serious wine-talk begins.*

Likewise two bottles can seem meagre for three people – they often feel like a third. Often four people need three, and can run to four. I have always supposed that the difference is accounted for by the energy you expend in conversation – that, and the time you spend over the meal.

Catering for a bigger party I usually assume that guests will somehow consume approximately one bottle of wine per head in total. This doesn't mean that I open that many bottles. I just make sure they're there.

And if wine is the main event, not supporting a meal but starring at a party with only canapés, or cheese, what then? For a start, choose a wine of moderate flavour and strength. Germany makes ideal wines for the solo spot, at every degree of sweetness, nearly always moderate in alcohol but in good examples wonderfully definite and clean-cut in flavour. They manage to keep your interest and go on being refreshing, without becoming too much of a good thing. But I must stress that I am talking about German quality wines, at least QbA level and preferably QmP, Kabinett wines.

Wines in the German style that achieve the same general effect, usually with two or three degrees more alcohol, come from Austria, north-east Italy (especially the Italian Tirol or Alto Adige), northern Croatia, parts of Hungary, and very notably from Australia. Barossa Valley Riesling from South Australia can be a great success at this sort of stand-up party. Among French wines I would choose the aromatic sort: Alsace's Edelzwicker or dry muscat or a Sauvignon Blanc from Touraine or Bordeaux or Poitou. I would tend away from Chablis or Muscadet or Mâcon Blanc which can become tiring to drink without food. Italy has dozens of very pleasant dryish white wines that score well at parties: notably Pinot Grigios from the northeast, Soave Classico, Frascati from Rome and Arneis from Piemonte. Spain's Penedès whites are also on about the right scale. The very light, slightly fizzy *vinho verde* of Portugal creates a certain exotic atmosphere but becomes faintly unsatisfying after two or three glasses.

I would not recommend California jug wines, except perhaps as a 'spritzer' or the base of a fruit cup – not such a terrible idea. A good Chenin Blanc or French Colombard could be acceptable, or a Riesling – if you can find one – better still. Chardonnay (and even Fumé Blanc) tend to be over-weighty for party drinking – at least to my taste. California wines are not on the whole as thirst-quenching as wines from Europe: an essential quality in a good party wine.

There are fewer reds that have the easy-going, refreshing, moderate degree of flavour that make them drink well over a period of time without food. The sort of tannin that makes deep-coloured young reds astringent turns your tongue and gums to leather after a bit. Beaujolais, rapidly fermented and only slightly tannic, flows well for a glass or two. Beaujolais-Villages flows better. Light young Côtes-du-Rhône reds are tolerable, but the sort of cherry-reds such as Valpolicella, Bardolino and Chiaretto of north-east Italy can be better. I stress the 'can'. There is a lot of rubbish sold under the name of Valpolicella. In California I would choose a light Zinfandel – not always easy to find – or an aromatic Pinot Noir.

The most valuable role of red wine at parties is in mid-winter, when it becomes the basis for what the British call mulled wine, the Germans *Glühwein*. The principle is simple: red wine mixed with orange and lemon juice (and zest), sweetened with sugar syrup, strengthened (this is optional) with brandy and spiced with cloves and cinnamon. It is a happy winter ritual, slowly simmering the wine in a huge pan, tasting as you go, adjusting the ingredients. Experience has taught me never to let the mixture boil, and to use an orange liqueur such as Grand Marnier in preference to brandy – added at the last minute.

The summer version of the same drink is Sangria: red wine and oranges, iced. So much watery and acidic liquid has been baptised with the name that I hesitate to mention how good it can be, freshly made with full-bodied red wine, sweet oranges, a little sugar and ice added only in large lumps.

The wine that is purpose-built for parties, though, is Champagne, or any of the countless sparkling wines made in almost every region today by the 'classic method'. The frivolity of fizz is its essential quality. It does not need to be the most expensive brand for a party – any party, even if you can afford it. Great bottles of luxury *cuvées* deserve to be kept for more intimate occasions.

Despite the recent wonderful improvement in quality of sparkling wines other than Champagne, people still sometimes hide the label of, say, a sparkling Saumur from the Loire or Crémant de Bourgogne, as though they were cheating their guests. Californians and Australians (and now New Zealanders too) know better and serve their native sparklers with pride.

For an afternoon party (which many weddings are) very dry Champagne is out of place. *Demi-sec* Champagnes are not usually as good, in my experience, as some of the

attractively fruity Crémants (top-quality sparklers) of the
Loire, Alsace or Burgundy, or a good German *Sekt*. Italian
and Spanish sparkling wines (the Spanish call the good ones,
generically, *cava*) tend to be made extremely dry – I am not
thinking of Asti-Spumante, the best really sweet fizz of all.

Someone fairly recently transferred to sparkling wine the
essentially tranquil idea of a great Burgundian priest and war
hero, the Canon Kir, who liked his dry, acidic white Aligoté
enriched with a drop or two of *crème de cassis*, the
blackcurrant cordial of his home town, Dijon. A 'Kir Royale'
is Champagne and *cassis*. Come to that, a 'King's Peg',
regal reviver of jaded professors at Cambridge University
(King's College claims the invention) is the same idea only
using vintage Champagne and a lovely old pale vintage
cognac as its ingredients.

*Above: A delicious party drink was invented at the turn of the century by the barman at Buck's Club in London, I believe. 'Buck's Fizz' is Champagne with fresh-squeezed orange juice. A 'Bellini' is the Venetian alternative: fresh-squeezed peach juice blended with the very dry sparkling Prosecco of the Veneto.*

# Tactics in the restaurant

*House wines and other gambits. Coping with a
wine list, ordering and testing a bottle, contending with
overbearing wine waiters and generally holding your
own when lunching or dining out.*

Whatever feelings of indecision you may have about
wine at home, they suddenly come to a head when you
go to a restaurant. An unfamiliar wine list and guests who
are thirsty put you on the spot. Traumatic confrontations
with wine waiters are almost part of folklore. But the popular
image of a wine waiter as an omniscient being breathing fire
and brimstone is very far from the truth. He often knows less
about wine than you do. It is the way he stands at your
elbow, a study in controlled impatience, that makes the wine
list seem endless.

Where is the best place to start? By asking for a copy of
the wine list with, or preferably before, the menu so that you
have time to size it up and settle on a strategy.

The conventional round of 'cocktails' gives you a few
minutes to get the measure of the list and some idea of the
restaurant's skill and interest in wine.

A very long wine list does not necessarily mean that
every wine is carefully chosen – or stored. It may have no
'depth' at all – just one bottle each of innumerable famous
wines which are replaced individually as (or indeed if) they
are sold. With a few celebrated exceptions, where wine is the
proprietor's genuine passion, very long lists can be regarded

**Above:** *Duel to the death or invitation to delight? Success with (and for) sommeliers comes through frank and open consultation. Professionals* *will steer you to parts of the wine list they know best and can guarantee value. The only secret is not to be hurried. Take your time.*

with suspicion. More impressive and reliable is the relatively short list which makes it clear that the person in charge has tasted and chosen all the wines and is prepared to take responsibility for them. A good wine list is fully specific about the origin of each wine: its vintage (never '1996/97' as though the year did not matter) and its producer. The name 'Chablis' alone means nothing. 'Chablis' with the name of a grower (whether you have heard of him or not) and a recent vintage is an indication that the list is compiled with a degree of care and revised regularly. If the list is vague, don't hesitate to ask to see the label of a bottle which might interest you – and reject it if it is not what you had hoped.

A restaurant wine list paints a rapid portrait of the knowledge and care (or lack of it) the management accords to wine. Here is a list of very uneven reliability, showing the kinds of points to watch out for.

*Lack of detail is the key wine-list sin. This means nothing. Whose Chablis? Which vintage?*

*From the Loire, which doesn't stop some restaurants from moving it to Burgundy.*

*This is the way to do it! Wine, status, vintage, producer – all clear to see.*

*Wide open to question. You would have to ask to see the bottle.*

*Is this German at all? Such made-up names can be Euro-blends.*

*Scarcely better: certainly German, but certainly a boring sweetish blend.*

*A fine vineyard and quality, but beware of the hedged vintage. And who made it?*

*Easy to dream up a name: but does it refer to anything more real than a marketing department?*

*Precise, well chosen producer, district, quality and vintage.*

# W i n e

## FRANCE

*White Burgundy*

Chablis

Sancerre

Chablis Premier Cru
Monts de Milieu 1996
Albert Pic

Meursault 1995

## GERMANY

Zellarblumchen

Liebfraumilch

Brauneberger Juffer
Riesling Kabinett 1995/6

## CALIFORNIA

Fog Bank Chardonnay 1997
North Coast

Cuvaison Carneros Reserve
Chardonnay 1996

# List

## FRANCE

### Red Bordeaux

Médoc

Margaux 1994

Château Bel-Air 1995

Château Fombrauge
St-Emilion 1990/91

### Burgundy

Beaujolais

Nuits-St-Georges
Pommard

Beaune Clos des Mouches
1995, Joseph Drouhin

## ITALY

Chianti Classico

## AUSTRALIA

Munnimunni Shiraz 1996

---

*Far too vague, but not necessarily a bad buy. Ask to see the producer/vintage.*

*Suspicious minds might decide this wine is here to deceive those who know there is a great château called Margaux. Ordinary AC Margaux will will probably be overpriced on this assumption.*

*A château – but which one? There are 30 'Bel Air's in Bordeaux. Without an appellation this could be any of them, from the famous to the obscure.*

*The vintage trap again: 1990 and 1991 St-Emilions are respectively excellent and indifferent. Which are you paying for?*

*Meaningless without producer or vintage. In any case straight Beaujolais without '-Villages' is rarely worth a restaurant listing.*

*These easy-to-pronounce names sell a lot of mediocre wine. It's crucial to know whose name is on the label.*

*Village, vineyard, vintage and grower/merchant. All we need to order with confidence.*

*The usual problem: no provenance or vintage.*

*Easy to disguise a cynical brand with an aboriginal-sounding name.*

# Opening gambits

A simple but effective dodge for establishing a bridgehead,
for getting an instant reference point on the capabilities of a
restaurant's wine buyer, is to order a glass of the house
white wine. A poor, flat or sharp house wine is a warning not
to pin too much faith on the rest of the wine list. A delicious
brisk and fruity one is an incitement to investigate what
other good things are on offer – or alternatively to order
more of the same.

There is a temptation to make an impression on entering
a strange restaurant by ordering Champagne. Apart from the
uplift of drinking it, the way it is served is another useful way
of gauging the competence of the cellarer. A good restaurant
has Champagne (not necessarily of every brand) already
cooled. A long wait followed by a great palaver with ice
buckets indicates that it is rarely asked for – and may well be
stored too long, in poor conditions. If (and it still happens
from time to time) the waiter brings shallow 'coupes' instead
of deep-bowled 'flutes' or 'tulips' don't hesitate to ask for the
restaurant's regular white wine glasses instead.

Champagne (as Sam Weller noted) can give you 'werry
gentlemanly ideas'. It also tends to give a restaurateur
certain expectations of you. To revert to a carafe of the
house wine afterwards is not only a gastronomic anticlimax;
it takes a modicum of moral courage too. My rule is to
behave in a restaurant as I would in an auction room: have a
clear idea of what I can reasonably afford to spend, given the
company and the class of restaurant, and then use the right
hand column to limit my choice to a comfortable level. I
probably survey the heights of the list, too. It is always a

pleasure even to read the name of Château Latour. But unless the company, the occasion and the restaurant are quite exceptional I would never dream of ordering the grandest wines in a restaurant, where they are marked up to at least twice, sometimes four or five times, their market value. The best place to drink the finest and rarest wines is in your own home.

## One wine or two?

On most occasions the choice of food will take precedence over the choice of wine. But this doesn't mean that wine need be an afterthought. The menu and the wine list are natural partners. There is time over a leisurely meal to enjoy at least two food-and-wine partnerships. The convention of drinking white wine first, and following it with red, is not only good sense for the wines but fits a wide range of menus.

What to do if one person in a party of, say, four or six has chosen a dish that really calls for white wine, while the rest would prefer red with the *daube de boeuf*? If the party has started with a bottle of white there may well be enough left for an extra glass or two for the fish-eater. If it has all gone, there is the alternative of ordering a glass or a small carafe of the house white, or a half-bottle of something more individual or of course for an experiment. I don't recommend Cabernet-based wines with most fish. Their tannin has unfortunate results. But young Pinot Noir/ burgundy can make a stimulating change.

Unfortunately most wine lists are lamentably weak in half-bottles even though restaurants are the very place where they can be most useful.

*Above: There is much to be said for relying on the host. Here at Olivier Leflaive's Table d'Hôte in Puligny-Montrachet the caviste pours a selection of the* négociant's *highly reputed burgundies to accompany the menu. The meal becomes a delightful learning experience.*

A couple dining together, and taking all evening over it, will usually find it no struggle to drink a whole bottle of wine. If a drink before dinner is included, it is quite realistic to think of two. If you have chosen different menus, there is no law that says you must compromise and drink the same wine. One of you can carry on with the white wine you had as an appetizer, the other can start a bottle of red – which you both finish with the cheese. It is always a mistake, though, to have wine as the only drink on the table: you will find yourself quenching your thirst with it, rather than enjoying it for its scents and flavours. Order a bottle or jug of water to drink alongside your wine. It will reduce your wine consumption by keeping your thirst at bay.

# Tasting the wine

You order a bottle. The waiter brings it to your table. He should show you the label, not just in courtesy, but to give you a chance to see that it tallies with the list. If there is a difference, in vintage date or producer, you have the option of accepting it or ordering another wine – which means another rummage through the wine list. For this reason I usually make a mental note of another wine on the list that I would settle for if my first choice turned out to be a dud.

For obvious reasons the cork and capsule should be in place when you first see the wine and the waiter should remove them in your sight. He then gives the host an inch or so of wine to taste, and will, in conventional restaurants, offer the cork as well. Ignore the cork and taste the wine. If it smells sweet and clean, all is well. If it smells mouldy, you have the one-in-sixty-odd bad luck of a 'corky' or 'corked' bottle. Sniff the cork: it will smell mouldy, too. It's the mouldy cork that has infected the wine. Nothing can be done except open another bottle, which a decent restaurant will do without demur.

But there are other ways in which individual bottles can occasionally go wrong. If a young white wine is yellowish or brownish and tastes flat (or if Champagne has no bubbles) you have a perfectly good reason for rejecting it. If the wine is a very old one it is at the discretion of the restaurant whether they will replace it. There is an old wine-merchants' saying, 'There are no great wines; only great bottles of wine'. But you should certainly say what you think. The proprietor would rather you came again than tell your friends they were mean. If on the other hand the taste is simply not what you were expecting, the lesson is at your expense – unless you are on very good terms with the management, or you are ready for a long discussion.

The question of temperature is entirely at your discretion. Many restaurants bring an ice bucket to keep white wine cool as a matter of course. The first sip will tell you whether it is cold enough for your liking. If it is (and some restaurants serve white wines too icy to taste properly) you can ask the waiter to leave the bottle on the table. (In hot weather it is wise to leave it in the bucket.) Refill you glasses from it when you like, notwithstanding the fuss that some waiters make in rushing up to pour for you.

## To decant or not to decant

Few restaurants seem to have a fixed policy about decanting red wine. I suspect they size up the customer before deciding. With many it is yes with Bordeaux, no with burgundy. There åre still unfortunately restaurants that bring on a decanting basket or cradle and serve the bottle from it; a certain recipè for muddy wine, with all the sediment stirred in each time the bottle is tipped. Be firm. Never let a waiter pour into glasses from a cradle. If the wine needs a cradle it needs decanting. Otherwise it should be stood upright.

If you choose a wine that you would decant at home, either because it has sediment, or you believe it would improve with aeration, ask the wine waiter to decant it for you. If he raises an eyebrow, or looks surly or sheepish, it may be because he is pressed for time, or possibly because he is not proud of his decanting skills.

In these circumstances you may quite reasonably say that you are prepared, or would prefer, to decant it yourself. Ask for the bottle in a cradle, a carafe and a candle. Let the waiter open the bottle for you in the usual way, while you discreetly sniff the carafe to make sure it is clean and fresh. Then take the bottle and decant it, being careful to leave the dregs. Remember the watchword: you are buying the wine; you can do what you like with it. Keep it under your control. But respect a wine waiter who clearly knows his job. Happily they are a multiplying breed.

# Glossary

# A

**acetic**
Unless wine is protected from the oxygen in the air its bacteria will rapidly produce volatile acetic acid, giving it a faint taste and smell of vinegar.

**acidity**
Don't knock it. At least half a dozen different acids are essential for zest, freshness, liveliness, aroma, longevity – the best wines have plenty of acid balanced by plenty of stuffing. You taste too much acid in poor wines because the stuffing is missing.

**aftertaste**
The flavour that lingers in your mouth after a sip. Scarcely noticeable (and occasionally unpleasant) in a poor wine; deliciously haunting in a great one. (*See caudalie.*)

**age**
Not necessarily a good thing. Cheap wines in general want drinking young. *See page 55.*

**alcohol**
Between 7 and 25 percent of a wine is alcohol, with most table wines in a range from 10·5 to 13·5 percent. During fermentation all or some of the sugar in the grapes is converted into ethyl alcohol, which acts as a preservative and gives the wine its 'vinosity', or winey-ness.

**Allier**
*Département* of central France just north of the Auvergne whose oak is in great demand for barrel-making.

**amontillado**
A matured fino sherry, naturally (and best) dry but often sweetened to be mellow in taste.

**American oak**
American oak, with a stronger and sweeter scent than most European oak, is in demand for maturing certain wines; for example Rioja.

*Above: The barrel, far from being an anachronistic container, plays a large part in the production of modern wine. Different oaks are used to add flavour like seasonings.*

*Appellation d'Origine Contrôlée* (AOC). Official rank of all the best French wines, meaning 'controlled designation of origin', shortened to *Appellation Contrôlée* (AC). On a label, this guarantees both place of origin and a certain style – though not, I'm afraid, quality.

**aroma**
The primary smell of a young wine, compounded of grape juice, fermentation and (sometimes) the oak of a barrel.

**astringent**
Dry quality, causing the mouth to pucker – the result of high tannin or acid content.

## *Auslese*
German for 'selection'. Refers to a category of QmP (*qv*) white wine made of grapes selected for ripeness above a statutory level, depending on the region. A good Auslese benefits from ageing for several years in bottle.

# B

**balance**
The all-important ratio between the different characteristics of a wine, such as fruitiness, sweetness, acidity, tannin content and alcoholic strength. These should harmonize like the various sounds in a symphony.

**balling**
*See* brix.

**Balthazar**
A monster Champagne bottle, equivalent to 16 ordinary bottles.

**barrel**
A vital part of the stabilizing and early ageing process for most of the world's best wines. New oak barrels are now routinely used for adding the strong scent of oak to 'premium' wines – not always with entirely happy results.

*barrique*
The standard Bordeaux barrel, holding 225 litres (49½ gallons).

**basket**
*See* cradle.

*Beerenauslese*
German for 'grape selection'. A category of QmP (*qv*) wine, sweeter and more expensive than Auslese because only the ripest bunches are used. Ages admirably.

**beeswing**
A kind of deposit sometimes found in port, so called because of the veined pattern it forms.

*Bereich*
A large area, although smaller than a 'region', in Germany. Bernkastel and Johannisberg are *Bereich* (as well as village) names, greatly increasing the quantity of wine available under these fashionable names – but of course doing nothing for its quality.

**bin**
A section of a cellar devoted to one wine – hence 'bin-ends' for oddments on sale.

**bitterness**
A taste not usually found in good wines – although some young tannins can be bitter – but a characteristic aftertaste of many north-west Italian wines.

**blackcurrants**
A smell and flavour characteristic of wines made from Cabernet Sauvignon and sometimes Sauvignon Blanc grapes.

**blend**
Nearly every wine involves some blending, whether it be of grapes, vintages or the contents of different vats. With fortified wines blending is almost universal. But blends of wines from different regions or countries tend to lack a distinctive character. (Some Australian blenders would disagree.)

**bodega**
Spanish word meaning a large storage vault, a wine-producing establishment or a bar.

**Botrytis cinerea**
The so-called 'noble rot', a mould that has the effect of concentrating the sugar and flavouring substances in grapes by allowing the evaporation of the water in the juice. Under controlled conditions it is used to produce sweet white wines of the highest quality (for example in Tokay and Sauternes).

*Above: Bunches of grapes affected by botrytis slowly desiccate as their skins are consumed by the mould. Eventually they become shapeless masses of dusty-dry raisins, intensely flavoured and as sweet as sugar.*

**botrytized**
Affected by the botrytis mould. A regrettable American neologism.

**bottle-age**
The length of time a wine has been kept in bottle (rather than in cask).

**bottle-sickness**
A (usually) temporary setback in a wine's flavour for weeks or months after bottling.

**bottle-stink**
A bad smell, which almost instantly dissipates, sometimes found on opening old bottles. It can be confused with 'corkiness' – but only for a few minutes.

**bouquet**
The characteristic smell of a matured wine, by analogy with a posy of flowers. Strictly speaking not the same as aroma (*qv*).

**breathing**
What wine is doing when you expose it to the air by decanting it a few hours before drinking. Opinions are divided as to whether wine benefits. *See pages* 35–7.

**breed**
A certain kind of polish and distinction in a wine. Found only in impeccably made wines from very good vineyards. A rather difficult word to use without feeling foolish.

**brix**
An American measure of the sugar content in grapes – hence the potential alcohol in wine. Formerly known as balling.

**brut**
Extremely dry. Usually used only in connection with Champagne.

**bunch thinning**
The selective removal of some of the ripening grapes in order to concentrate the flavour and colour of the remaining crop.

**butt**
A sherry or whisky cask that holds 491 litres (108 gallons).

# C

**carafe**
Stopperless container used for serving wine at table. The 'carafe wine' ('jug wine' in the US) in a restaurant is the standard house wine.

**cask**
Another term for a wooden barrel used for storing wine or spirit. Casks come in many sizes and have different names depending on what they contain. A sherry cask is a 'butt'; a port cask is a 'pipe'.

***caudalie***
French measure of the length of time the aftertaste of a wine lasts.

***cave***
French for cellar.

***chai***
Storage building of a château or wine estate (especially in Bordeaux) where wine is kept in cask.

***chambrer***
French word meaning to bring (wine) from cellar- to room-temperature. *See pages* 37–9.

***chaptalization***
The French term for the addition of a small permitted amount of sugar during fermentation in order to boost the alcoholic strength of a wine.

**character**
Term of praise indicating that a wine has its own distinctive and individual stamp.

**château**
Used in a wine context, this means either the country house or mansion of a wine-producing estate or the estate as a whole. Where it appears on a French label it means that the wine comes solely from that estate.

**château-bottled**
Bottled on the estate rather than by the merchant. Other things being equal, château-bottled wines are generally more highly valued, whether or not their quality justifies it.

**chill**
*See pages* 37–9.

**claret**
English term for the red wines of Bordeaux.

***classé***
French word meaning 'classed'. There have been many classifications of the vineyards of France, the most famous that of certain Bordeaux châteaux in 1855. Each important area of France has its own 'classed growths', or their equivalents, but there is no unifying system. The term is most often used about Bordeaux.

***classico***
Italian for 'classic', referring to the core of a DOC region. *Metodo classico* on sparkling wine is the legal term for what used to be called 'Champagne method'.

***clavelin***
A dumpy, old-fashioned bottle used in France's Jura.

**climat**
Burgundian word for an individual
vineyard site.

**colour**
*See pages* 44–5.

**commune**
The French for parish. Many wines
bear the name of a parish rather
than that of an individual grower
(for example St-Julien, St-Emilion,
Pommard).

**cooperage**
A general term for wooden
containers or the workshop where
they are produced. A cooper is a
barrel-maker (and a rich man
these days).

*Above: In the past many wine companies
made their own barrels. Today barrel-making
is largely in the hands of five or six French
specialists. Most barrels are shipped abroad
as green wood staves to be seasoned, bent
(by being steamed, immersed in boiling
water or 'toasted') and assembled on the spot.*

**cork**
*See pages* 9–13.

**corkage**
Charge made by a restaurant to
those who bring their own wine.

**corky or corked**
Wine contaminated by a rotten
cork, resulting in an unpleasant
smell and taste.

**coulant**
'Flowing'. French term for easy-
to-drink wines such as Beaujolais.

**coulure**
A condition of the vine at flowering
time, causing the grapes to fall off
prematurely.

**courtier**
French term for a wine broker.

**cradle**
A device for holding a bottle in a
near-horizontal position so that it
can be opened and poured without
the deposit being disturbed,
properly used only for decanting
purposes. The basket fulfils a similar
function.

**crémant**
Now a controlled French
appellation for the sparkling wines
of certain quality regions, notably
the Loire, Alsace and Burgundy.

**cru**
French word for 'growth', applied to
the produce of a vineyard or group
of vineyards making wine of a
particular character.

**crust**
A heavy deposit found particularly
in bottles of vintage port.

**cuvée**
The contents of a *cuve* (vat). It
can also mean a quantity
of blended wine.

# D

**decant**
To transfer wine from a bottle to a stoppered flask (decanter). *See pages 34–7.*

***demi***
Half.

**demijohn**
A type of large bottle, usually encased in wickerwork and holding at least 4·5 litres (one gallon). The name probably derives from the French *Dame Jeanne*.

***demi-sec***
French for 'half-dry'. The term is usually applied to sparkling wines and means that sugar has been added to produce a degree of sweetness, sometimes marked.

**deposit**
High-quality wines maturing in bottle almost always develop a greater or lesser deposit, the fall-out from chemical changes which give them greater character, complexity and bouquet.

**disgorge**
Refers to the classic method of making sparkling wines. At one point the bottle has to be opened to remove a deposit of yeasty sediment. In French *'dégorgement'*.

**DOC**
*Denominazione di Origine Controllata* (controlled denomination of origin). An Italian classification, similar to the French AOC but here more a bureaucratic control than an assurance of quality.

**DOCG**
The top category of Italian wines, theoretically superior to DOC (*qv*) as indicated by the addition of the letter G for *garantita* (guaranteed).

**domaine**
A (wine-producing) property. This is the normal word in Burgundy, whereas in Bordeaux they use the term 'château'.

**dosage**
The sweetening added to sparkling wine before the final corking.

**double magnum**
A four-bottle bottle containing three litres (5 ⅓ pints) of wine – the same capacity as Champagne's equivalent, a Jéroboam(*qv*).

**dry**
A relative term, implying the opposite of sweet.

# E

***Einzellage***
German term meaning a single, individual vineyard site, as opposed to a *Grosslage*, which refers to a collection of such sites.

***Eiswein***
Very sweet German wine made by harvesting frozen grapes during a frost and pressing them while they are still frozen. The flavours and acidity are intensely concentrated and the wine apparently almost immortal.

**elegant**
As of a woman, unmistakable but indefinable.

**éleveur**
Someone who buys new wine from the grower and prepares it (or 'brings it up') for sale.

**enology**
*See* oenology.

**Erzeugerabfüllung**
Literally 'producer-bottling'. The German equivalent of 'domaine-bottled'.

**extract**
Soluble solids from the grape which contribute to the weight and fullness of a wine: the components of its flavour.

# F

**Fass**
German for cask.

**fermentation**
The conversion of grape juice into wine through the action of certain yeasts present on the skins which turn sugar into alcohol. *See also* malolactic fermentation.

**feuillette**
A Chablis barrel.

**fiasco**
A Chianti flask. The traditional straw jacket is now more often made of plastic.

**fine**
A general term of approbation denoting overall quality.

**finesse**
Literally 'fine-ness'. The word implies subtlety and distinction.

**fining**
Clarifying wine by pouring on a coagulant (such as egg whites or blood) and letting it settle.

*Above: You can't fine the finest wines without breaking eggs. The whites of many dozens are whipped up and poured into barrels to 'polish' the wine as they sink to the bottom.*

**finish**
The final taste left by a sip of wine on swallowing.

**fino**
The finest style of sherry – dry, delicate and usually light in colour. Finos should be drunk as fresh as possible, and never kept in an opened bottle.

**fliers**
Little specks of sediment.

**flute**
A tall, narrow, cone-shaped glass, perhaps the prettiest for sparkling wine.

**fortified**
Strengthened by the addition of extra alcohol during production.

**foxy**
Tasting of native American or 'fox' grapes.

### *frais*
French term meaning either fresh or cool.

### *frappé*
French for very cold or iced.

### *frizzante*
An Italian term meaning slightly sparkling, as opposed to *spumante* which is fully sparking.

### fruity
Tasting pleasantly of ripe grapes – but a term so widely used as to have little clear meaning.

### *Füder*
Type of cask, holding about 960 litres (211 gallons), used for Mosel wine.

### full or full-bodied
Refers to a wine that is high in alcohol and extract, causing it to feel weighty and substantial in the mouth.

### *fumé*
Literally 'smoky'. The term refers to the peculiar tangy aroma of certain young wines made from the Sauvignon Blanc, for example Pouilly Fumé.

### *fût*
General French word for a cask.

# G

### *garrafeira*
Portuguese term for merchant's selection – frequently his best long-matured wine.

### *gazéifié*
French for fizzy or carbonated.

### generic
In California, the opposite of 'varietal', for example wine called 'Burgundy' or 'Chablis' is 'generic', while those labelled 'Pinot Noir' and 'Chardonnay' are 'varietal'.

### Grand Cru
Literally 'great growth'. Means different things in different regions of France. In Burgundy it is the top rank. In Bordeaux (particularly St-Emilion) almost everything is a 'Grand Cru'. In South Africa, for some reason, it can refer to a cheap white wine.

### *Grosslage*
In German terminology a group of neighbouring *Einzellages* (*qv*) of supposedly similar character.

### *Gutsverwaltung*
German for property or estate.

# H

### harmony
A highly desirable quality: a balance of attributes.

### hock
Now archaic British term for the white wines of the Rhine and surrounding areas. It is believed to derive from Hochheim, a town on the River Main.

### hogshead
A cask. The size and contents vary depending on where the word is being used. A hogshead of Bordeaux wine, also known as a *barrique*, contains 225 litres (49½ gallons), whereas one of whisky holds 248·2 litres (54¼ gallons).

**hybrid**
Used in wine circles of a cross between French and American vines, designed for hardiness. Hybrids are much used in the eastern USA and sometimes in England.

# I

**impériale**
Outsize Bordeaux bottle, holding about eight standard bottles, occasionally used for very fine wines.

# J

**Jéroboam**
Champagne bottle size, with the capacity of four normal bottles. In Bordeaux a 'Jéro' holds six normal bottles.

**jug wine**
Otherwise known as 'carafe wine', '*vin ordinaire*' or 'plonk'. Cheap, workaday wine without pretensions.

# K

*Kabinett*
The first category of *Qualitätswein mit Prädikat*, the highest classification of German wine. Kabinett wines are lighter and less expensive than other QmP wines such as Spätlese and Auslese.

*Kellerabfüllung*
Bottled at the (German) cellar.

**kosher wine**
Wine for Jewish religious occasions, made under the supervision of a rabbi. It is usually very sweet.

# L

*lagar*
The stone trough in which the grapes are (or were) trodden by barefoot workers to make port and other Portuguese wines.

*Lage*
German term for a particular vineyard.

**lees**
Solid residue remaining in the cask after the wine has been drawn off.

**legs**
The rivulets that run down the side of a wine glass after the wine has been swirled around it. When the legs ('church windows' in Germany) are pronounced it indicates a wine rich in body and extract.

**light**
Possessing a low degree of alcohol or, more loosely, lacking in body. Desirable in some cases, most German wines for example, but not where something more intense or weighty is required.

**Limousin**
Region of north-central France whose oak forests produce strongly-perfumed wood for barrels.

**liquorous**
Used of wine that is rich, sweet and pretty strong. In French, *liquoreux*. Sauternes is the classic example.

**litre**
Bottle size used mainly for everyday wines. The standard capacity of a wine bottle is 75cl (1⅓ pints).

# M

### maderized

The term refers to the brown colour and flat taste of a white wine that has been over-exposed to air during production or maturation to the extent that it smells or tastes like Madeira.

### magnum

Wine bottle holding 1·5 litres (2⅔ pints), the equivalent of two normal bottles.

### malolactic fermentation

A secondary stage of fermentation in which malic acid is converted into lactic acid and carbon dioxide. As lactic acid is milder, the taste of the wine becomes less acid. Some winemakers encourage it, if necessary, by warming the new wine. Others avoid it to keep a sharper acidity.

### marc

The pulpy mass of grape skins and pips left after the fermented grapes have been pressed. Also the name of the strong-smelling brandy distilled from this.

### *marque*

French for brand. In Champagne the '*grandes marques*' are the top dozen or so houses.

### *méthode champenoise*

The 'Champagne method'. Formerly used world-wide to signify the laborious way of making sparkling wine perfected in Champagne, but now outlawed in favour of the words 'classic method' or local equivalents.

### Methuselah

Not an unusually long-lived wine but a bumper Champagne bottle with a capacity equivalent to that of eight normal bottles.

### *millésime*

French for the vintage year (for example 1998).

### *mise*

French word meaning 'putting', used for bottling. The past participle occurs in such phrases as *mis en bouteille au château* (château-bottled). But sometimes you will see simply *mise du château*, meaning the same thing.

### *moelleux*

French for 'marrow-like'. Used of a wine it means soft and rich, particularly of Loire wines such as Vouvray that vary from dry one year to *moelleux* the next.

### *monopole*

A wine whose brand name is the exclusive property of a particular firm or grower.

### *mousseux*

French for sparkling. Not usually used for first-class wines.

# N

### Nebuchadnezzar

The largest size of Champagne bottle, holding the equivalent of 20 ordinary bottles (*see picture overleaf*). Named after the colourful king who destroyed Jerusalem and built the Hanging Gardens of Babylon. He would doubtless have appreciated the tribute.

*Above: Left to right: a quarter bottle of Champagne, a Nebuchadnezzar (the Sumo size: 20 bottles) and a standard 75cl bottle. The very useful pint size, alas, has been banned by Brussels.*

### négociant
French term loosely translated as 'shipper', but implying a dealer who buys wine from the estates and distributes it either wholesale or retail. *See also éleveur.*

### nerveux
A term of praise implying fineness combined with firmness and vitality.

### noble rot
*See Botrytis cinerea.*

### nose
Wine jargon for smell, whether aroma or bouquet (*qqv*).

### nouveau
As in Beaujolais Nouveau – the wine of the last harvest, in its first winter.

# O

### oaky
Refers to a wine that has picked up something of the taste and smell of the oak cask in which it was matured. Many producers go to great trouble to obtain the right nuance of oakiness by choosing oak of a certain type for their barrels. *See* Allier, American, Limousin, Tronçais.

### Oechsle
System used in Germany for measuring the proportion of sugar in the must.

### oeil de perdrix
'Eye of the partridge', a metaphor used to describe the pink colour of certain rosé wines as well as some pink Champagnes and even whites with a pinkish tinge.

### oenoconomy
Counting the change (if any).

### oenology
Knowledge or study of wine (from the Greek *oinos*, wine).

### oenophile
A lover or connoisseur of wines.

### oloroso
A natural style of sherry classified as 'pungent' (as opposed to 'fine'). With age it becomes the noblest, nuttiest, most memorable of all.

### organoleptic
A high-falutin way of saying 'sensory'. Organoleptic evaluation is the judging of a wine by measuring its effect on the different senses.

### Originalabfüllung

The German equivalent of *mis en bouteille au château*. It means 'original bottling' and signifies that the wine has been bottled on the premises by the grower. *Originalabzug* means the same.

### oxidized

Possessing a stale, flat taste owing to excessive exposure to air. *See also* maderized.

# P

### palo cortado

A rare and excellent style of sherry, between fino and oloroso (*qqv*).

### passito, vino

Strong, sweet Italian dessert wine made from grapes that are dried, traditionally on straw mats, for a brief period before being pressed.

### pasteurization

Process invented by Louis Pasteur (1822–95) in which substances are sterilized by heat. It is used for certain run-of-the-mill wines, but it is not considered desirable for the finer ones.

### pelure d'oignon

Onion skin. This is how the French describe the pale, orange-brown colour of certain rosé wines and some old reds.

### perlant

Showing a slight degree of sparkle, much less than *mousseux* (*qv*).

### Perlwein

German name for a wine that is *pétillant*.

### pétillant

Having a very light, natural sparkle, even less pronounced than that of a *perlant* wine.

### phylloxera

An American vine pest accidentally introduced into Europe in the latter part of the 19th century. It destroyed almost all vineyards; not only in Europe but throughout the world with a few exceptions such as Chile, in a disaster without precedent. Most vines world-wide are now grafted onto American phylloxera-resistant stock.

### pied

French for a single vine.

### pipe

A port cask containing 522·48 litres (115 gallons). The word is also used to refer to a Madeira cask containing 418 litres (92 gallons) and a Marsala cask holding 422 litres (92⅔ gallons).

### plastering

Not getting someone drunk, but boosting the acid content of a wine by the addition of calcium sulphate (plaster of Paris). The practice is more common in Mediterranean countries (especially in making sherry) where the natural acid content of the wine tends to be low.

### 'plonk'

Slang for everyday wine, possibly a garbled version of blanc, as in *vin blanc*.

### porón

Double-spouted Spanish drinking vessel which enables the wine to be drunk without the glass touching the lips. When the glass is raised one spout lets out a stream of wine while the other lets in air.

**port**
English name for the fortified wine produced on the banks of the Douro River in northern Portugal and matured in the cellars at Vila Nova de Gaia. It is made in both red and white forms.

**pot**
A type of fat-bellied wine bottle now largely confined to Beaujolais.

**pourriture noble**
See *Botrytis cinerea*.

**Prädikat**
See QmP.

**Premier Cru**
First of the five categories of Médoc châteaux established by the classification set up in 1855 which comprises Château Lafite-Rothschild, Château Latour, Château Mouton-Rothschild, Château Margaux and Château Haut-Brion. But in Burgundy the term refers to the second grade of classed vineyard (the first is Grand Cru).

**premium**
California term for wines over a certain fairly modest price – the opposite of 'jug'.

**pricked**
A useful, if archaic, term for the unpleasantly sharp quality caused by the presence in the wine of too much volatile acidity.

**primeur**
Term applied to certain wines sold very young, especially Beaujolais.

**punt**
The hollow mound poking up inside the bottom of a wine bottle. Universal in old hand-blown bottles but now generally limited to Champagne and port.

# Q

**QbA**
Abbreviation for the term *Qualitätswein eines bestimmten Anbaugebietes* (quality wine from a specific region), the second-highest category of German wine. QbA wines are closely delimited in their origins but are made of grapes that ripened insufficiently to make wine without added sugar – as distinct from the next category, QmP.

**QmP**
*Qualitätswein mit Prädikat* (quality wine with special attributes), the top category of German wine, made with only fully ripe grapes. QmP wines are subdivided into five further categories: Kabinett (light and usually fairly dry), Spätlese (fuller and usually fairly sweet), Auslese (rich and usually sweet, sometimes superbly honeyed), Beerenauslese and Trockenbeerenauslese (*qqv*).

# R

**racking**
Transferring the fermented wine from one cask to another to separate it from its lees (*qv*).

**ratafia**
Brandy mixed with sweet
unfermented grape juice, also
available as Pineau des Charentes.
A speciality of Champagne.

**récolte**
French word for the harvest, crop
or vintage.

**Rehoboam**
Another of those biblical names for
big Champagne bottles. This one
holds the equivalent of six normal
bottles.

**remuage**
Technique invented by the widow
Clicquot in the early 19th century
for removing the deposit in
Champagne without removing the
sparkle. It involves shaking and
turning each bottle and inclining it
at a progressively sharp angle until
it is almost upside down (*see
picture, page* 59). This goes on for
six weeks or more until all the
deposit has settled on the cork.
Then the cork is taken out (*see*
disgorge) and the deposit
extracted.

**reserva**
Italian term for wine that has been
aged for a statutory period, its
length depending on the DOC (*qv*).

**réserve**
An uncontrolled French term
implying superior quality.

**Rhenish**
Archaic term for Rhine wine.

**riddling**
English term for *remuage* (*qv*).

**riserva**
Spanish equivalent of *reserva* (*qv*),
with similar statutory limits. *Gran
riserva* is the highest official
category.

**rosato**
Italian for rosé.

**rosé**
Pink wine made from black
grapes pressed quickly to allow only
some of the skin-colour to tinge the
wine. Rosés vary in colour from
deep pink, almost red, to pale,
almost white.

**rosso**
Italian for red.

**rouge**
French for red.

**ruby**
The name given to young red port,
darker and fruitier than tawny, that
has aged in wood for two to three
years.

**rurale, méthode**
Probably the original way of making
sparkling wine, antedating the
*méthode champenoise*. Still used,
with modifications, in Limoux in
south-west France.

# S

**sack**
Archaic term for sherry and similar
strong wines.

**Salmanazar**
The third-largest size of Champagne
bottle, holding the equivalent of 12
normal bottles.

**Schaumwein**
German for sparkling wine.
No implication of quality.

**Schillerwein**
A type of German rosé wine, made
from a mixture of black and white
grapes. The name comes from the
word *Schiller* meaning lustre and
has nothing to do with the poet
Schiller.

**Schoppenwein**
The 'open' wine sold in a German
*Weinstube* or tavern.

**sec**
In French this word means dry
or fermented out, but in relation to
Champagne it is used in a
somewhat specialized way. A very
dry Champagne is described as
'brut'. *Sec* means containing some
added sweetness. *Demi-sec* means
decidedly sweet. With other wines
the word *sec* is an indication of
relative rather than absolute
dryness. The same applies to the
Italian word *secco*.

**secco**
*See sec.*

**sediment**
Solid matter deposited in a bottle in
the course of the maturing process.
Nearly always a good sign.

**Sekt**
The German word for sparkling
wine.

**solera**
The name for a system of blending
and maturing sherry, also applied to
the storage building where the

process takes place. The sherry is
arranged in different casks
according to age and character, and
the contents of the casks are
transferred and blended in complex
permutations that vary from one
firm to another.

*Above: The barrels (they are called butts)*
*in a sherry* solera *remain in place, often*
*stacked five high, while the wine is transferred*
*from one to the other by either hoses or*
*gleaming cans.*

**sommelier**
French term for a wine waiter.

**sparkling**
Containing bubbles of carbon dioxide
gas. This condition can be brought
about in three different ways:
(1) fermentation in the bottle
(Champagne or 'classic' method);
(2) fermentation in a closed vat
(Charmat method); (3) pumping $CO_2$
into the wine (rudely called the
Bicycle Pump method).

**Spätlese**
German term for a wine made from
late-harvested grapes.

**spritzer**
A drink made with white wine
diluted with soda or mineral water.

**spritzig**
German adjective describing a wine with a light, natural sparkle.

**spumante**
Italian for fully sparkling.

**stuck**
Of fermentation: the point where, owing to an uncontrolled rise in temperature, the yeasts are overcome by the heat and the fermentation stops.

**Stück**
The traditional 1,200-litre (264-gallon) cask of the Rhine.

**sulphur**
The most common disinfectant for wine. It is dusted onto the vines to prevent fungus, burnt inside casks to fumigate them and added to the must, usually in the form of sulphur dioxide, to destroy harmful bacteria. Unless it has been carelessly used the flavour of the sulphur will not be transmitted to the wine.

**süss**
German for sweet.

**Süssreserve**
Unfermented, and therefore naturally sweet, grape juice. Used in Germany to blend with dry wines to balance them.

# T

**table wine**
In common use, this means any non-fortified wine. In EEC terms it means a wine below the rank of *Vin de Qualité Produit dans une Région Déterminée* or VQPRD (*qv*).

**Tafelwein**
*Deutscher Tafelwein* is the lowest of the three categories of German wine. The presence of the word '*Deutscher*' indicates that the wine is made entirely in Germany. If it is called simply *Tafelwein* it may be blended with wines from other countries.

**tannin**
A substance found in the skins, stalks and pips of grapes. It is also absorbed into wine from oak casks and is sometimes added artificially. Tannin acts as a preservative and is therefore an important ingredient if the wine is to be matured over a long period. In excess it imparts a hard, dry quality. But fine ripe tannins contribute the essential, satisfying, 'structure' of a wine in the mouth.

**tappit-hen**
Pewter vessel holding 4.1 litres (7¼ pints), formerly widely used in Scotland. Alternatively, a port bottle with the capacity of three normal bottles.

**tartaric**
An acid occurring naturally in grapes and the main constituent of the acidity in wine.

**tastevin**
Shallow vessel of silver, glass or ceramic, used in Burgundy for sampling wine. Its shape, with indentations and a raised boss in the centre, makes it easier to judge the colour of a wine in a dark cellar.

**tasting**
*See* Judging wine, *pages 43–9*.

**tawny**
The name given to port that has been aged in wood until it has acquired a tawny colour.

**temperature**
*See pages* 37–9.

*terroir*
A French word meaning soil and site in their ecological totality. A wine is said to have *un goût de terroir* (a taste of the soil) when it has gathered certain nuances of taste and flavour from the land on which it was produced.

*tête de cuvée*
A term used mainly in the Burgundy area to refer to the 'cream' of the wine sold under a particular name.

*tinto*
Spanish for red.

*tirage*
French word usually meaning the transfer of wine from cask to bottle. Literally 'drawing off'.

*Tischwein*
German for table wine. Not an official term (*see Tafelwein*) but used to refer to ordinary mealtime wines.

*tonne*
French for a large cask or container of unspecified size.

*tonneau*
A general French term for a cask, but in Bordeaux it refers to a quantity of wine, namely 1,000 litres, or 100 cases.

*trocken*
German for dry. Trocken wines are often good with food in the QbA and Spätlese categories.

*Trockenbeerenauslese* (TBA)
A category of German wine. It is made by picking out individual grapes affected by the noble rot, *Botrytis cinerea*, which produce an exceptionally rich, luscious (and expensive) wine.

**Tronçais**
France's finest oak forest, in the Allier (*qv*). Twenty-five thousand acres of great trees giving fine-grain subtly scented oak which is used for the very best wine barrels.

**tun**
Archaic term for a barrel.

# U
**ullage**
The amount of wine that would be needed to top up a bottle (or barrel) right to the cork (or bung). 'Ullaged' bottles (with empty necks) can be disappointing.

# V
**varietal**
A varietal wine is one that is named after the grape variety from which it is made. 'Varietal' is an adjective, 'variety' the noun.

**vat**
Large vessel or tank for fermenting or blending wine. Nowadays vats may be made of wood, concrete or stainless steel, sometimes with a glass lining.

**VDQS**
(*Vin Délimité de Qualité Supérieur*) The second official category of French wines, subject to slightly less rigorous regulations than those applying to *Appellation Contrôlée* wines. The category was set up in 1949 and has since become firmly established.

*vendange*
The French word for vintage.

*vendemmia*
The Italian word for vintage.

*vignoble*
French for vineyard.

*vin de garde*
A wine whose potential to mature makes it worth keeping.

*vin de l'année*
Literally 'wine of the year', that is to say of the current vintage.

*vin de la région*
What you ask for when you want a wine made in the region where you happen to be.

*vin de liqueur*
This is the French name for what in Britain would be called 'fortified wine', a term which in France would imply an improper addition of alcohol.

*vin de paille*
A (now rare) way of producing sweet wine with a mild but fresh and lively taste by drying the grapes on straw (*paille*) mats before crushing and fermenting them. Usually marketed in half-bottles.

*vin de pays*
Not to be confused with *vin de la région*, this is the third official category of French wines, established in 1976. The wines are now innumerable, some large (*vin de pays de zone*), some covering *départements* (*vin de pays départementale*), some (the most interesting), small districts.

*Vin Doux Naturel*
(VDN). A description used for a type of wine made in southern France. These wines are high in natural sugar and are fortified by the addition of extra alcohol, making them about as strong as an average sherry. Drink them as dessert wines, after meals or on their own, like sherry.

*vin jaune*
These are white wines with a yellowish hue caused by bacterial action during the long fermentation process. They have a strong and distinctive flavour and bouquet and are made solely in the Jura region of France. The best is known as Château Chalon.

*vin nouveau*
New wine, made to be drunk just after the vintage. Beaujolais is the most famous, but many other French regions now market a *nouveau*.

*vin ordinaire*
Not an official category of French wine but a loose term for basic wine, bought often by the alcoholic degree per litre and regarded as a grocery commodity, not a subject for connoisseurship.

**viña**
Spanish for vineyard.

**vinho generoso**
Spanish term for aperitif and dessert wines such as sherry.

**vinho verde**
A light, tangy wine made in northern Portugal. The name, meaning 'green wine', refers to its newness, not its colour. It comes in both red and white, but the term is mainly associated with the white version.

**vintage**
The annual harvesting and production of a wine. More particularly, a vintage wine is one that bears the date of the vintage on the label, either because it is meant to be drunk young or because it was made to be matured over a number of years.

**viticulture**
The science and art of growing grapes.

**VQPRD**
*Vin de Qualité Produit dans une Région Déterminée* (quality wine produced in a defined zone). This is an EEC quality category. Italian DOC, French AOC and German QbA (*qqv*) wines all qualify. In the eyes of Brussels, all else is just 'table wine'.

# W

**Weingut**
Term used in Germany and Austria for a wine-producing estate that grows its own grapes.

**Weissherbst**
A type of white wine made in Baden, Germany, from black grapes.

**Winzergenossenschaft**
The German word for a wine cooperative, a group of growers who have clubbed together to produce wine.

# Y

**yeast**
A collection of micro-organisms that cause fermentation (*qv*). Wild yeasts are naturally present on grape skins, but artificially developed yeasts are used by most modern winemakers (except the best).

**yield**
The amount of wine produced by a vineyard, usually expressed in hectolitres (100 litres) per hectare or hl/ha. Higher quantity means lower quality or lighter wine that matures more rapidly.

# Index

Page numbers in italic
refer to captions and
illustrations.

## A

acidity 36, 55, 64, 98
aeration 35, *45*, 46
aftertaste 81–2
age 35, *45*, 55, 98
alcohol *46*, 60, 68, 76,
  77, 98
Aligoté 56
apertif wines 56, 57, 76–9
Argentina 58, 61
Arneis 85
aroma 41, 46–7, *47*, 98
Asti Spumante 60, 79, 87
Ausbruch 62, 79
Auslese 30, 58, 62, 71,
  79, 99
Australia 52, 57, 59, 61,
  62, 66, 68, 84
Austria 58, 61, 62, 84

## B

Bardolino 64, 85
Barsac 61
Beaujolais 64, 85
Beaujolais Nouveau 21
Beaune-Clos des
  Mouches *91*
Beerenauslese 62, 99
Bellini *87*
Blanquette de Limoux 59
blush wines 63
body *48*
Bonnezeaux 62
Bordeaux 28, *29*, 36,
  64, 66, 68, 96
  white Bordeaux 56
botrytis *29*, 100, *100*
bouquet 36, 47, 100
Buck's Fizz *87*
Bulgaria 61
burgundy 28, *29*, 35, 66,
  68, 70, 73, 93, 96
  white burgundy 30, 60

## C

Cabernet Franc 63
Cabernet Sauvignon *29*,
  45, *52*, 63, 64, 66
California 52, 56–7, 58,
  59, 61, 62, 63, 66, 68, 85
Carneros *90*
*cassis* 56, 87
*caudalie* 81, 101
*cava* 59, 87
cellar 21–5, 32, *33*
  non-traditional solutions
    24–5
  spiral cellar 23–4, *24*
  temperature 22–3
cellar mould *22*
cellar records 25–7, 32–3
Chablis 30, 56, 70, 84, 89
*chambrer* 39, 101
Champagne 13, 59, *59*,
  63, 75, *75*, 77, 80, 86,
  92, *108*
Chardonnay 46–7, 60, 72,
  76, 85
Château Margaux *19*, *50*
cheese, wine with 61,
  71, *71*
Chenin Blanc 58, 60, 85
Chianti 64, *65*, 66
Chiaretto 64, 85
Chile 52, 61, 66
chocolate, wine with 72–3
climate 53–4, *53*
Colombard 58, 85
colour 28–30, *29*, 44–5
cork oak *9*, 10
corks and other closures
  9–13
  broken/immovable/
    pushed in corks 8, 10,
    15–16
  capsules 11–12, *11*
  keeping moist 10, 23
corkscrews 12, *14*, 15
corky/corked wine 10–11,
  95, 102
Coteaux du Layon 62
Côtes-du-Rhône 85
cradles 96, 102
Crémant d'Alsace 59

Crémant de Bourgogne
  59, 86
Crémant de la Loire 59
Crémants 59, 86–7, 102
Crimea 62
Croatia 84
Cyprus 63

## D

decanters 34
decanting wine 12, 34–7,
  103
  in restaurants 96–7
Dolcetto 64

## E

Edelzwicker 84
end-of-dinner wines
  79–80
Entre-Deux-Mers 56
EuroCave 24–5, *25*

## F

Fendant 57
finish 49, 104
fish and shellfish, wine
  with 70, 72, 93
food, matching wine with
  56, 61, 69–74, *71*, *72*, 80
fortified wines 68, 104
France 56, 58, 59, 60–2, 63,
  64, 65, 68, 84, 85, 86–7
Frascati 56, 61, 85
Fumé Blanc 85
Furmint 60

## G

Gaillac 56
game, wine with 71
Germany 57–8, 59, 62,
  77, 84
Gewürztraminer 58, 60, 62
glasses 39–42, *40*
  coupes 39–40, 92
  flutes 92, 104
  Paris goblet 42
  regional designs 42
*Glühwein* 85–6
grape varieties 52–3 (*see
  also* individual entries)

# Picture Acknowledgements

**6** Reed Consumer Books Limited/Jeremy Dixon **9** Reed Consumer Books Limited/Alan Williams **11** Reed Consumer Books Limited **14** Reed Consumer Books Limited **17** top left Reed Consumer Books Limited **17** top right Reed Consumer Books Limited **17** bottom left Reed Consumer Books Limited **17** bottom right Reed Consumer Books Limited **19** Cephas Picture Library/Mick Rock **22** Cephas Picture Library/Mick Rock **24** The Spiral Cellar – Cave Harnois **25** EuroCave **26** Reed Consumer Books Limited **29** top left Reed Consumer Books Limited/Steven Morris **29** top right Reed Consumer Books Limited/Steven Morris **29** bottom left Reed Consumer Books Limited/Steven Morris **29** bottom right Reed Consumer Books Limited/Steven Morris **31** Reed Consumer Books Limited **33** Reed Consumer Books Limited/Sally Cushing **34** left Reed Consumer Books Limited/James Johnson **34** right Reed Consumer Books Limited/James Johnson **37** Hugh Johnson **40** Hugh Johnson **43** Eduard Rieben **45** left Reed Consumer Books Limited **45** right Reed Consumer Books Limited **46** Reed Consumer Books Limited/Steve Tanner **47** left Reed Consumer Books Limited **47** right Reed Consumer Books Limited **48** left Reed Consumer Books Limited **48** right Reed Consumer Books Limited **50** Cephas Picture Library/Mick Rock **52** Cephas Picture Library/Mick Rock **53** Cephas Picture Library/Mick Rock **54** Root Stock/Hendrik Holler **56** Reed Consumer Books Limited/Steven Morris **57** Reed Consumer Books Limited/Steven Morris **58** Reed Consumer Books Limited/Steven Morris **58** left Reed Consumer Books Limited/Steven Morris **59** Cephas Picture Library/Mick Rock **60** Reed Consumer Books Limited/Steven Morris **61** Reed Consumer Books Limited/Steven Morris **63** Reed Consumer Books Limited/Steven Morris **64** Reed Consumer Books Limited/Steven Morris **65** bottom Reed Consumer Books Limited/Steven Morris **65** top Cephas Picture Library/Mick Rock **66** Reed Consumer Books Limited/Steven Morris **67** top Reed Consumer Books Limited/Alan William **67** bottom Reed Consumer Books Limited/Steven Morris **68** Reed Consumer Books Limited/Steven Morris **71** Anthony Blake Photo Library/Tim Imrie **72** Cephas Picture Library/TOP/Pierre Hussenot **74** Cephas Picture Library/Mick Rock **75** Anthony Blake Photo Library **78** Anthony Blake Photo Library/G. Buntrock **83** Anthony Blake Photo Library **87** Anthony Blake Photo Library **89** Cephas Picture Library/TOP/Pierre Hussenot **94** Cephas Picture Library/Mick Rock **98** Cephas Picture Library/Mick Rock **100** Root Stock/Hendrik Holler **102** Root Stock/Hendrik Holler **104** Root Stock/Hendrik Holler **108** Cephas Picture Library/Mick Rock **112** Cephas Picture Library/Mick Rock